The
Fast Forward
MBA in Technology
Management

THE FAST FORWARD MBA SERIES

The Fast Forward MBA Series provides time-pressed business professionals and students with concise, one-stop information to help them solve business problems and make smart, informed business decisions. All of the volumes, written by industry leaders, contain "tough ideas made easy." The published books in this series are:

The Fast Forward MBA in Technology Management
   (0-471-23980-1)
   by Daniel P. Petrozzo

The Fast Forward MBA in Hiring
   (0-471-24212-8)
   by Max Messmer

The Fast Forward MBA in Business
   (0-471-14660-9)
   by Virginia O'Brien

The Fast Forward MBA in Finance
   (0-471-10930-4)
   by John Tracy

The Fast Forward MBA Pocket Reference
   (0-471-14595-5)
   by Paul A. Argenti

The Fast Forward MBA in Marketing
   (0-471-16616-2)
   by Dallas Murphy

The Fast Forward MBA in Technology Management

DANIEL P. PETROZZO

John Wiley & Sons, Inc.

New York • Chichester • Weinheim • Brisbane • Singapore • Toronto

Published by John Wiley & Sons, Inc.
Published simultaneously in Canada.

This publication is designed to provide accurate and authoritative
information in regard to the subject matter covered. It is sold
with the understanding that the publisher is not engaged in
rendering legal, accounting, or other professional services. If
legal advice or other expert assistance is required, the services of
a competent professional person should be sought.

Library of Congress Cataloging-in-Publication Data:
Petrozzo, Daniel P.
    The fast forward MBA in technology management / Daniel P.
Petrozzo.
        p.   cm.
    Includes index.
    ISBN 0-471-23980-1 (paper : alk. paper)
    1. Information technology—Management.
2. Manufacturing industries—Management.   3. Customer
services—Management.
    I. Title.
    HD30.2.P483   1998
    658.4'038—dc21   98-2775
                                                         CIP

Printed in the United States of America.

10 9 8 7 6 5 4 3 2 1

To my children,
Nicole and Michael.

CONTENTS

Daniel P. Petrozzo is a Principal at Morgan Stanley Dean Witter & Co. He has over 14 years' experience in the information technology (IT) industry. Previously, he worked as an independent consultant to many industries on issues related to strategy, reengineering, IT, and business development. He is the coauthor of a prior book, *Successful Reengineering*.

The Pace of Change

The *pace of change*—we are constantly hearing about the manic pace of change in our lives. Two-family incomes, 100 cable stations, sprawling suburbia, soccer moms, all leading to more complicated, action-packed days. Because it is almost self-evident, it is rather trite to point out that technology is a key driver in moving along this rate of change. Technology has permeated almost every aspect of our daily lives, from on-line banking to the constant pursuit of new video games for the children. But as pervasive as technology has become in everyday society, the impact on businesses is even more dramatic. Just ten years ago, although around for awhile, the PC was hardly existent in most companies. Now, everyone seems to have at least one on his or her desk. Once personal computers were stand-alone; now they are networked and internetworked. The Internet was a mere tool for some wacky people reading newsgroups and sending electronic mail. Now it is mainstream—what advertisement on television doesn't read "www" on the bottom? I think the point is clear. Computers and other forms of technology, from fax machines to robots, are here, and they are not going away anytime soon.

The proliferation of high-technology products and services offers an insight into how many companies across industries are investing in technology products, and it provides valuable lessons for managers on how to run and grow a business in the most volatile, competitive marketplace to date.

In the late 1980s and 1990s, businesses experienced a spate of new management approaches—most notably, downsizing and reengineering. This era completely changed how we work and, for many, where we work. Today the globalization of companies and dramatically increased worldwide competition force many businesses to be 24×7 operations mandating increased communication across a diverse workforce. At the root of many of the new ways that companies compete, enter markets, keep in touch with customers, and work in extended partnerships is technology. For us mere mortal managers out there, understanding various technologies and creating management strategies that effectively make use of the company's systems presents yet another difficult challenge to contend with.

THE REACTION FROM THE BUSINESS SIDE

Although we are probably being led by the most technology-savvy CEOs to date, it's fair to say that the heads of companies are typically not technologists by training. Nevertheless, they have become forced to react to the impact of technology in their businesses. Technology is no longer to be thought of as merely a cost required to support isolated business functions such as payroll, order entry, and accounts payable. Rather, technology spending and computer literacy for many companies are becoming increasingly part of the overall corporate agenda to be used to greatly improve the internal operations of companies, penetrate new markets, supercharge sales initiatives, and develop innovative products.

At the most senior levels, technology is becoming a factor in the way companies think. Recently, MCI sponsored a survey where 555 CEOs were queried as to what advice they would give to others trying to ensure that their businesses would remain competitive. Although the usual tips were offered, including improving customer service and innovation in producing products, a significant number of them pointed out that keeping up with new technologies would become increasingly important. Notable facts in figures include that 44 percent of the CEOs believe that information technology (IT) or communications capabilities will be the technology trends that will most help their businesses over the next five years, and 66 percent believe that in five years, doing business on the Internet will be critical to staying competitive.[1]

High-technology companies themselves are learning how to manage the rapid pace of their volatile landscape and stay competitive within their own marketplaces through management and technology strategies designed to suit their businesses. Throughout the book, in sections titled "Stellar Performer" and "Fast Forward to the Real World," you will read about the thinking and strategies that keep these companies afloat.

Another indication of how business executives view the role of technology in their companies is the increasing reliance of the chief information officer (CIO) in company-wide decision making. Over the years, there has been quite a bit of debate about the reporting relationship of the CIO. In the old days, technology, like operations, was considered a cost center—not adding to the bottom line. This began the days in which the person that managed in the information systems division reported to the chief financial officer. Today, many companies have the CIO report directly to the CEO or president of the company. The reason for this is that technology needs to be discussed as a strategic topic on the corporate agenda. The reason for this is twofold. First, technology expense (including such items as telecommunications) is often the largest budget item that a company has. Second, most core businesses (e.g., trade processing at a securities firm) are dependent on technology performing properly every single day.

Businesspeople have embraced the idea that technology is a force that influences both strategy and operation, and its importance in the workplace will only continue to grow. Technology will be a part of each business decision that managers will have to make, and technology innovation will be more valued than ever.

GOALS OF THE BOOK

The purpose of this book is to enlighten the business manager on the issues regarding the management of IT. Just the fact that it is time to

dedicate a book to this subject suggests the importance that IT has gained in business and society.
This book is for all those managers out there who
need to deal with the volatile technology landscape. It is for the managers who need to figure
out how to use technology to make their businesses operate better, or in some cases, at all.
We'll examine a wide range of topics, from how to
manage technology projects and people across
various industries, to the effects that all of this has
had on the people using systems day in and day
out. In addition, we'll offer perspectives and expe-
riences from the field about how companies are
actually applying technology. It is a very real and
compelling fact for managers that technology
strategy is now a dominant agenda item for most
companies.

Fast **F**orward to the Real World

Lester Thurow: An Interview with Eric Nee

Eric Nee

Spend a few hours in the office of Lester Thurow, professor of management and economics at the MIT Sloan School, and you know you're back in academia. His office in Cambridge, Massachusetts, overlooking the Charles River, is cluttered with books and papers. Students drop in from time to time. A well-used Macintosh computer sits on his desk.

Yet Thurow is more than an ivory-tower theoretician. His thinking, expressed in such books as *The Zero Sum Society*, has influenced economists and policy makers worldwide. A known Democrat in what is generally viewed as a conservative profession, Thurow has undoubtedly found credence within the Clinton administration, especially for his views on the interrelationship of social and economic structure.

Fast-talking, with a tendency to ramble, the tall and lanky Thurow bears a slight resemblance to the 1960s singer Art Garfunkel (though with less hair). Outside the office, the 55-year-old Thurow is an avid outdoorsman, having climbed several of the world's highest mountains, such as Alaska's Mount McKinley and Pakistan's Gasherbrum II. Just after doing this interview, he was on his way to Canada's Hudson Bay region to observe polar bears in the wild.

In talking with *Upside*, the renowned economist expounded on Japan versus the United States, government's proper role in the information highway, and numerous other topics.

UPSIDE: **Economically, which region of the world is better off, and which is worse—Japan, Europe, or the United States?** THUROW: The interesting thing today is, if you go around the world and talk to people, everybody will tell you that they live in the country with the worst economic problems. From an objective point of view, the country in the worst shape is Japan. They've got the biggest negative real growth. In the United States, we had a banking crash and a property crash; the Japanese had a banking crash, a property crash, and a stock market crash. Very few Ameri-

(Continued)

(Continued)

can newspapers have commented on the fact that after you correct for inflation and deflation, in percentage terms the Japanese stock market has gone down more than the American stock market did from 1929 to 1932. You've got every company in Japan losing money and market share. In our world, companies at least know how to handle that—you lay people off. But in Japan, they don't know how to handle it because, one, you don't lay people off and, two, if you did lay people off, that isn't laying people off, that's changing the whole Japanese social structure. So the country that has done the best over the last 30 years has done the worst over the last two years and is in the most severe recession of any part of the world.

In Europe they have had their trials and tribulations, but in the end, the Maastricht treaty was passed by all 12 [European Community] countries. They have all committed themselves now to a common currency by the year 2000. So I don't think the Europeans will, in the end, throw it away through ethnic animosity.

If you look at the United States in terms of economic growth, we're the best-performing part of the world, but we've got some very fundamental educational and social problems that aren't being addressed.

Why is the world economy having such difficulties? Since the speculative bubble of the 1980s, we have wiped out on a worldwide basis hundreds and hundreds and hundreds of billions of dollars of wealth. That's got to have some impact on somebody. And another thing we did in the '80s which we're absorbing in the '90s is we produced enormous excess capacity. For things like automobiles, computers, and airplanes, the world could produce two or three for every one it's going to buy. The other day a newspaper mentioned that Tokyo now has more empty office space than the total in Boston plus San Francisco. We've got whole cities full of empty office buildings. You're not going to go out and build an automobile plant; you're not going to build a computer plant; you're not going to build an aircraft factory. I would describe the current period not as a recession, but as a period of cleaning up the mess at the end of the speculative bubble after a substantial financial crash.

Since World War II, Japan's whole economic model has been built on rapid growth and exports. They had an economy that couldn't take recessions and that's why they didn't have recessions. Recession in Japan was in the first derivative. If growth slowed down, that was a recession—not if growth went negative. But now they've had two years of negative growth and no end in sight.

(Continued)

(Continued)

What kind of an impact will that have on their social structure, which you call "communitarian capitalism"? Do you think that is threatened? Oh sure, it's threatened. Because, basically it was a private social welfare system. But you can't run a private social welfare system unless the private companies can generate the resources to pay for it, and they can't generate the resources to pay for it unless you get economic growth.

In the United States we can deal with that more easily than they can in other countries. Our companies are the world's best at downsizing because America is the easiest country in the world to fire people. In places like France, you've got to give a year's notice and two years' wages, which means you've got to pony up to the table three years of wages before you can lay somebody off. That's a very expensive process, and you are going to do it very reluctantly.

The problem in the United States is we make it very easy for the private economy to deal with the downturn and we essentially throw all of the problems into the social sector. Then you get all of this urban violence and chaos among young men with no jobs—that shouldn't really come as a great surprise, should it? You know, if you were a 20-year-old man with no prospects of making a living, what would you do? Probably the same things they are doing.

You've held up Europe and Japan as models for the United States. Do you think that is still the case? I think it's still the case, but I think the real issue here is going to be, in this difficult decade of the '90s, what's the system that can get through it best. Looking at the social structure, it's not obvious we are going to make it at all. But if you look at the companies, you would say they are in more trouble in Japan than they are in the United States. On the other hand, they don't have the kind of urban chaos that we have. So I don't know.

Of course one answer may be none of the above. One of the interesting things today is if communism had not collapsed, people would be writing articles about the collapse of capitalism. Because capitalism isn't delivering the goods. What unemployment rate have you got in Spain and Ireland? Something like 21 percent. That is not delivering the goods. In the United States, we have a much lower unemployment rate, but I was just digging the numbers out the other day: If you are a male in the bottom 60 percent of the population, from 1973 to 1992, the real per capita American GNP goes up 27

(Continued)

(Continued)

percent, and your wages, after correcting for inflation, go down 20 percent. So for that 60 percent of the population, capitalism hasn't delivered the goods. The goods is not just a job; the goods is a job with either constant or rising income. Europe has protected wages but produced these enormously high unemployment rates because no one wants to hire new people. The United States has let wages fall and then generated jobs. I don't know which is better or worse.

But fundamentally, within capitalism you have to have a strong private sector to support the social programs. Oh, absolutely. But see you've got the other side, too. To have a viable private sector, you've got to have a strong social sector in the sense that the government does the research and development. The government provides the infrastructure. The government provides the educated manpower. And of course, our government—in this case it isn't the federal government, it's local school boards—if you would rate our local school boards on their ability to produce world-class manpower, you would give them a flunking grade. Both sides have something very important they have to do.

Is lack of growth the fundamental economic problem, or is it that we are in the midst of—as some people in high tech like to say—the "information revolution"? I think we are in the middle of several revolutions. We're in a revolution in the world's trading system. After World War II, the system was designed for a world where you had a dominant trading partner: the United States. You no longer have that. It's collapsing in the Uruguay Round [of GATT]. And you also have some technological changes that allow you to manage things around the world better than you ever have before.

And you manage with fewer people? Fewer people, yes. But the intriguing thing is that the way economists measure technical change is with productivity growth. Productivity growth is not higher; it's lower. The rate of growth has fallen. In the '60s, world productivity was probably growing at 3.5 percent, but the world economy was growing at 5 percent, so you generated jobs.

Today, productivity has probably fallen to about 2.5 percent, but the world economy is growing at 1.5 percent, and so you lose 1 percent of jobs. So there is no evidence that technical change has speeded up. What you have to argue is that there may be some kind of a structural transformation, but not that it is occurring at a faster

(Continued)

(Continued)

pace. Because the objective evidence is that we are moving slower technologically today than we did in the '60s.

When do you see an upturn in the economy? I think the answer is nobody sees an upturn. One will eventually come, but the economic telescope goes only 18 to 24 months into the future, and the people who are in the professional forecasting business—that's not me—none of them sees an uptick worldwide.

Do you think that the U.S. economy will continue to grow at a rate greater than that of Europe or Japan over the next couple years? It certainly might. That would be the standard forecast.

Why is Europe not more competitive in industries such as semiconductors, software, computers? Chemicals, pharmaceuticals—that is where the action is. Who is buying whose high-tech drug companies? It's the Europeans buying the American start-ups. In aircraft, Airbus Industries has driven Lockheed out of the business, McDonnell out of the business, and is now taking market share away from Boeing. I think it's hard to know why they have been so bad in microelectronics. It's a bit of a mystery.

Could it have to do with the pace that the technology itself changes? Maybe. In aircraft, the technology to make a plane is reasonably well known, and it's a matter of amassing the capital and engineers to put it together. A lot of people in Europe have speculated about why they are so far behind in microelectronics, and nobody has come up with a good answer.

How important is that industry to an economy? It's very important. If you would ask "What is the hottest technological area?" I think it's this intersection of telecommunications, computers and visual images. And of course, when it comes to telecommunications, there the Europeans can claim to be the world leader. And so [technology] may be moving into an area where they have more strength than we do.

What do you think about that business in the United States? Well, I think we have a real problem in getting our act together and having a system. One of the strategic weaknesses of the American economy is we often have very good individual competitors and then have a lousy system which destroys everything. You see it

(Continued)

(Continued)

in the airline industry. We've got the most competitive airplane companies in the world, and they are all losing billions of dollars because we run a lousy system. You can be a genius running American Airlines and you're still going to lose millions.

The problem in telecommunications since we broke up AT&T is while we may have even better competitors than we used to, we still don't have a system. And the question is, in this race to build the information highway, how do you get it built when there is no system?

Do you think it's too fragmented? Yeah, everybody says, "I want you to build the highway, and I want to use it, but I don't want to have to help build the highway." And we have a law that says the guys who own the highways—the Baby Bells—at least until recently, couldn't participate in using the high value-added highway. Well, if I own the highway—the copper wires—I'm not going to upgrade them to fiber optics so you can make a lot of money, am I? I don't think so.

A lot of people have speculated that the cable companies will provide possible competition for the RBOCs. We had a little bit of bad luck in the sense that if cable had started 20 years later they would have done it all with fiber optics rather than coaxial cable and we'd be a hell of a lot better off. Both the telephone companies and the cable companies have buried a lot of obsolete technology in the ground.

Do you think the proper role for the government is in easing the regulatory path rather than funding it? They may have to do some funding, too. It depends on what kind of a regulatory framework you set up. If AT&T was a monopoly, then AT&T would do it without any government funding because it would essentially have a way to tax the public through the basic telephone rates. Given a competitive industry, you may very well have to have some government funding simply because there isn't any other way to do it. We could have private highways. Why don't we? The answer is it just isn't efficient. It's more efficient to have the government pay for the highways and then charge us indirectly through the gasoline tax.

U.S. companies seem to be investing heavily in new communication technologies without any government prodding. Doesn't mean that they will make the money on it, though. Who invented the video camera and video recorder? The Americans. Who

(Continued)

(Continued)

made the money on it? The Japanese. Who invented the fax? The Americans. Who made the money on it? The Japanese. Who invented the CD player? The Dutch. Who made the money? The Japanese. To say you are first at the ballpark isn't to say that you're going to economically dominate the industry.

There has certainly been a lot written about those failures. American companies would hopefully have learned something. But see, it isn't a matter of learning it down at the company level. It's a matter of learning it at the system level. To make this into a profitable industry, you have to have the system, and no individual company is going to build the system. The question is, can we get our act together and build a system?

Some U.S. companies have begun developing alliances with Japanese companies to leverage one another's strengths. Some of that makes sense, but I don't think the basic analysis is right. We're both very good where we concentrate our money and our talent. [In the late 1980s] American companies were putting two-thirds of their R&D money and their most talented people into inventing new products, and spending one-third of their R&D money on new processes and putting less talented people there. The Japanese were doing exactly the opposite: two-thirds of the R&D money and the most talented people went into process technology and one-third of the money and the less talented people into product technologies. And surprise, surprise—we're both very good where we concentrated our money and talent.

I don't think Americans have any advantage in inventing new products and I don't think the Japanese have any advantage in running factories. If we put our talented people into running factories and put twice as much money into equipment, which is what they were doing, we'd run very good factories. If they put all of their talented people and a lot of money into inventing new products, they would invent new products.

Given that that's where we are today, do you think it makes sense for companies like 3DO to say, "Okay, we'll invent the technology and then we'll contract with Matsushita to make the thing"? Oh, it might make sense for the individual company, but it doesn't make sense for the society because the jobs are where you build the products, not where you invent the stuff.

(Continued)

(Continued)

Is there any evidence that U.S. companies are getting better at manufacturing? Absolutely. The best example is the automobile companies which, partly through the good luck of having Americans all want to buy pickup trucks but partly by building a better product, have reduced the Japanese market share from around 32 percent to 27 percent over the last couple of years. And most of the people who study the automobile industry say American car companies are now producing a car equal in quality to that of the Japanese.

Do you see any evidence that the Japanese are focusing more on innovation? They've come to the conclusion that, at least in some industries, they've got to learn to be more inventive. The best example is consumer electronics. The Japanese have been too good in consumer electronics. They have driven everyone else out of the business, and therefore nobody is thinking up new products. Which means the Japanese have got to think them up. The '80s were a boom decade in consumer electronics because you had three hot new products: video recorders and video cameras, faxes, and CD players. In the '90s, thus far they haven't come up with a new product the public wants.

The convergence of computing and consumer electronics may provide a way for U.S. companies to get back into that market. If the whole thing moves to digital, that gives American companies certain advantages. The problem in consumer electronics is that you've got to have a brand name, which is a very expensive thing to establish. The famous American brand names have all been sold to foreigners—RCA, General Electric, Zenith. And so even if you invent a product, how are you going to sell it? A smart start-up can invent a product, but then you may need $700 million to do the advertising.

Hewlett-Packard is one company that might be able to do that. They are beginning to build and sell their own fax machines. Sure. If you look at their little hand calculators, they have been in that business for a long time. And at the high end, I suspect they have a good market share.

What about software? That's almost a quasi-American monopoly.

(Continued)

(Continued)

Is it likely to stay that way? I was just reading some of the information that's been coming out about the potential suit by the Justice Department against Microsoft. In prepackaged software, Americans have 75 percent of the world market. In total software, including custom design systems, American companies have about 50 percent of the world market. Based on that you'd say, sure, they are going to keep it. The problem is, all you need is about 15 guys with a hot idea and they might be the new Microsoft. It's an industry that is too easy to break into. You see, Intel is in a much stronger position than Microsoft because Intel tells us that it will spend roughly $5 billion for R&D and manufacturing over the life cycle of the Pentium. The next chip will cost more, so if you don't have $5 billion, you are not going to get into the microprocessor game. How much money do you need to get into the computer software game? Approximately zero.

You've written about the fact that the use of computers in white-collar jobs hasn't really had much effect. It seems not to have paid off. Although in the last 12 months—which doesn't make a trend yet—there seems to be a little uptick in productivity in the white-collar service area. Maybe it just takes 15 years for people to figure out how to do it. [Laughs]

Were people doing it wrong? You had all of these mysteries like when we computerized accounting, right? And we doubled the number of accountants. Now why did we do that? Well, we created all kinds of new accounting—we started inventory control accounting, cost accounting, financial accounting, etc. Instead of closing the books once every three months, we close them every night. The fact that we were doing all of these new things meant that you had to add twice as many accountants to the economy, even though you were computerizing accounting. Maybe we learned what pays off, and we quit doing some of these things. One of the problems we have in the United States is there is a real technologic drive—if you can do it, you must do it. But there are a lot of things you can do that don't make any sense to do. They are technologically possible but irrelevant.

The consultants promoting reengineering say the problem was businesses were overlaying new technology on old processes. There was some truth to that. People used the phrase "automate the office," which meant you were going to

(Continued)

(Continued)

march in and do exactly what you had always done, but just automate it. That clearly is never the right thing to do. If you've got a new technology, you've got to do it in new ways, but that means new power and authority relationships. With the word processor, you shouldn't have a secretary, right? But it's very hard for a company to take secretaries away from the top brass. Because secretaries are more than somebody who does your typing or filing; they're a mark of status.

Until recently most layoffs involved blue-collar workers. But in the last year you see a lot more layoffs of middle management, which is what you would expect if you used the technology. The technology is there to skip layers of management. And when you can electronically interact with each other, you don't need 5,000 people at corporate headquarters.

It seems that U.S. companies are doing that kind of shifting more than European and Japanese companies. I think that's right. Partly because the Japanese have never had as many layers of management. We can lay off a lot of managers before we get down to the Japanese level. And partly because in both of those places it's much harder to fire people, or even move them from one job to another.

You've said that U.S. businesses need to learn to operate as groups. In high technology, the idea of alliances is becoming popular. Will alliances make U.S. companies more competitive? If you can make them work in the long run. There have been waves of interest in these joint things, and then they all peter out because they don't work. To make them work, you've got to have joint ownership and then work out some real, cooperative framework. In the United States, if you look at any joint operation and then come back 10 years later, you find one partner has bought out the other partner, or one partner has become a silent financial partner and the other partner really runs the show. Very seldom do you still see genuine cooperation.

Are companies going to repeat those mistakes? From the outside it's very hard to say. Both sides have to see working together in the long run as better than working separately. And that's only true as long as you are both getting something from working together.

(Continued)

(Continued)

Do you think that might change because of convergence?
The computer companies can't do it alone; the entertainment companies can't; the communications companies can't. It's going to be interesting to see if these alliances win out or whether simply people buying each other wins out.

Source: excerpted from Eric Nee, "Lester Thurow: An Interview with Eric Nee," Upside magazine (January 1994).

Editor's Note: Thurow is still at MIT. His latest book is The Future of Capitalism: How Today's Economic Forces Shape Tomorrow's World *(Morrow, 1996). Eric Nee, formerly editor of* Upside *magazine, is now Silicon Valley bureau chief for* Forbes *magazine.*

CHAPTER 1

The Value of Technology to Business

Information technology can and does create value for most businesses. However, industry pundit Paul Strassman realized a long time ago that the computer, in and of itself, provides businesspeople with very few answers. As Strassman noted, "A computer is only worth what it can fetch at an auction. It (IT) only has value if surrounded by appropriate policy, strategy, methods for measuring results, project controls, talented and committed people, sound organizational relationships, and well-designed information systems. . . . The productivity of management is the decisive element in whether a computer helps or hurts."[1]

In essence, a company can only realize value from technology if it figures out ways to leverage it to make money.

At this point, it is fairly safe to say that nothing has impacted the business landscape over the last decade as much as technology. A multitude of interrelated factors have led to this rampant change. Some of these factors are driven by the technology industry itself, whereas others are consequences of new global economic forces. We examine each of them below:

1. Moore's Law was invented by Intel Corporation founder Gordon Moore. Moore's Law states that computer processor chips will double in capability every one-and-a-half years. For the most

part, this has occurred over the last ten years, and companies such as Intel show no signs of slowing down in making processors faster, smaller, and cheaper. The availability of powerful computers that can be run from a desktop has had tremendous impact on business. Computers now become obsolete quickly, and companies need to spend additional money buying new ones and retraining their staff. Software developers are able to take advantage of the new hardware and develop larger, more sophisticated computer programs that can be run by the end user. These new systems drive important functions within the business, including research and development (R&D), customer care initiatives, and internal company communications.

2. The need for worldwide, near-real-time communications is a chicken-and-egg story. Did companies need to become global and far reaching for competitive advantage, or did the technology companies creating communications capabilities develop the need by offering the capability? Regardless, at this point, to fuel growth and to reach far-away markets, more and more companies rely on around-the-clock communications and data transfers with their far-flung operations. This is evidenced by the proliferation of telecommuters, virtual workers, and outsourcing operations.

3. The increased number of technology initial public offerings (IPOs) and venture capitalists is another factor. Technology (IT, as well as others, like biotechnology) has found its way into the hearts and wallets of venture capitalists and other investors. Silicon Valley has become synonymous with the new land of opportunity in a California-Gold-Rush fashion. Further, the technology industry fuels the need for more technology, as it has become a significant factor in the total economy. The heads of companies such as Oracle, Microsoft, Sun Microsystems, Intel, and Cisco are extremely powerful and wealthy, as are their companies. This leads to a serious ability for a few technologists to create and move markets for products as well as financial markets.

4. The Internet is the final factor. Not unlike dog years, Net years have taken society by storm. It

was only a few years ago that the Internet was not even heard of, much less a serious factor in how people work, companies communicate, and products are sold. Now the Internet is a household word and considered by many the next consumer medium. This has caused every industry to react in some way and try to keep pace with Net developments as they rapidly emerge.

This change in events has expanded the role of technology management, from the realm of a few decision makers concerned only with preserving the firm's data center, to the forefront of the executive's agenda. It is now—and is becoming increasingly—unsatisfactory for corporate managers to ignore or merely delegate technology decision making to others. One of the key reasons for this is the fact that technology budgets for most companies are growing at a fairly rapid pace. At the same time, there are other key changes in our society that are making this an issue for all managers. The Generation Xers and the Generation Nexters are coming into the workplace with computer skills and ideas on how computer systems can help them achieve the jobs they do. This, of course, is outside of those that find their way into the technology organization. At the same time, the popularity of the Internet has made electronic mail and browsing a growing part of the fabric of society. Furthermore, the success of companies like Microsoft and Intel and their role in the stock market have made the average investor acutely aware of the role of technology in society. The average investor once could easily understand that McDonald's makes burgers, but now they go a quantum leap further to find out that it is Cisco that "provides all these funny boxes that keep the Internet humming."

TECHNOLOGY MANAGEMENT IS DEFINED BY A SERIES OF ACTIVITIES

What is technology management? Much like other well-known things that we have been exposed to, such as reengineering and quality management, there is no single definition for technology management. So, let's try to establish a working definition to frame the remainder of this book.

Technology management cannot be defined in a simple sentence. Instead, it is defined by a series of functions or activities.

- Managing the life cycle of technology in a business, including evaluation, selection, development, implementation, purchasing, and disposal. This is a responsibility often shared between the business people in a company, as well as the technology department.

- Managing and interfacing with the people (including external vendors) that do the activities in the preceding point.

- Managing the business you are in with an eye toward how technology can create competitive advantage, be a barrier to entry to a particular business, be similar to a utility, or improve operational efficiency.

END POINTS

Technology management is a very important aspect of what a manager needs to do in any business. Few business decisions can be made without understanding the implications they will have from a technology perspective, and, in some cases, the decisions themselves can only be made by using technology.

The Top 25 Techno-MBAs

Managing technology is growing increasingly important. In addition to churning out the next generation of financiers, marketeers, and consultants, business schools are increasingly focused on issues relating to technology in business. In 1997, *ComputerWorld* published a list of the top 25 MBA programs for information systems management. It surveyed more than 3,000 recruiters at large- and medium-size corporations and 304 deans of MBA programs. The surveys asked recruiters to rate which programs produce strong information systems leaders, managers, entrepreneurs, and consultants. Deans were asked to rank the top MBA/IS programs.

Rank The Top 25 Schools

1   Massachusetts Institute of Technology, Cambridge, MA (617) 253-5049

2   University of Texas at Austin, Austin, TX (512) 471-5240

3   Carnegie Mellon University, Pittsburgh, PA (412) 268-8933

4   University of Minnesota, Minneapolis, MN (612) 624-4519

5   University of Michigan, Ann Arbor, MI (313) 763-9779

6   University of Illinois at Urbana-Champaign, Urbana, IL (217) 244-8019

7   University of Arizona, Tucson, AZ (520) 621-2748

8   University of Pennsylvania, Philadelphia, PA (215) 898-8036

9   University of California at Berkeley, Berkeley, CA (510) 642-1425

10   New York University, New York, NY (212) 998-0844

11   Texas A&M University, College Station, TX (409) 845-4711

12   Purdue University, West Lafayette, IN (317) 494-4366

13   Indiana University, Bloomington, IN (812) 855-8489

14   University of Rochester, Rochester, NY (716) 275-3316

15   Georgia State University, Atlanta, GA (404) 651-3871

16   Georgia Institute of Technology, Atlanta, GA (404) 894-8713

17   University of Pittsburgh, Pittsburgh, PA (412) 648-1561

18   Rensselaer Polytechnic Institute, Troy, NY (518) 276-2033

19   University of California at Irvine, Irvine, CA (714) 824-8470

20   Ohio State University, Columbus, OH (614) 292-2666

21   The University of Georgia, Athens, GA

(Continued)

(Continued)

22   University of Wisconsin at Madison, Madison, WI
23   Florida State University, Tallahassee, FL (904) 644-8213
24   Arizona State University, Tempe, AZ (602) 965-5516
25   Boston University, Boston, MA (617) 353-3366

Source: ComputerWorld *(On-Line Features, 19 May 1997).*

Fast
orward to the Real World

Leveraged Buyout Firms Go Tech

Jim Evans

Two decades ago, during the technology revolution's infancy, leveraged buyouts (LBOs) in IT would have been inconceivable. Technology we take for granted, such as chip manufacturing, was then regarded as an unpredictably weird science in an industry composed of engineers whose machinations fell just short of witchcraft. But the high-tech industry has matured, and as evidence, non-high-tech LBO firms have begun buying technology companies to round out their holdings. High tech is such a big part of the economy, these firms say, that it's natural for the LBO companies to want a piece of the action.

"High tech is becoming so pervasive that it's difficult to stay out of the market," says Brian Baer, a partner at Deloitte & Touche LLP in San Jose. "As the tech industry as a whole matures, there are sectors of it that are known markets . . . at the low end of the tech arena."

In the past year alone, Sterling LLC, a Citicorp venture capital investment firm, bought an equity stake in chipmaker Fairchild Semiconductor; Kohlberg Kravis Roberts & Co. acquired interconnect maker Amphenol Corp.; and Texas Pacific Group bought chipmaker Zilog, Inc.

Leveraged buyouts that invest so-called dumb money in high tech have, in a way, replaced shareholders; only now, the cash providers have a direct say in how a company spends its money—if they want it. That hasn't been the case at Fairchild, says Kirk Pond, president and CEO of the South Portland, Maine–based company, where Citicorp, which owns 63 percent of Fairchild, has, for the most part, let the company run itself.

"Our industry has been basically financed by nontech money," Pond says. Although he acknowledges that the trend of mature companies being bought by LBO firms is relatively new, Pond says the relationship works for Fairchild. "The method of operation fit where we wanted to take the company," he says. "They are not managers of companies, they are investors in companies. They are long-term players, and this is patient money."

(Continued)

(Continued)

It had better be. The chip industry has been characterized by short product life cycles that can force companies to change direction in midstream. To overcome the inherent unsteadiness of the business, LBO firms look for established players that make products that are not highly technological and that possess established distribution channels.

But Ernest Ruehl, senior vice president of Lehman Brothers, which represented Zilog in its deal with Texas Pacific Group, warns of the potential for disaster. "There's just so much money out there," Ruehl says. "Whether people do something stupid soon is another thing." What would be stupid? "Overpaying and putting too much debt on a company that has limited and risky technology," he says.

Pond agrees that a nontech LBO firm buying a high-technology company is sometimes considered too risky, because the industry is cyclical. But a company with "multimarket chip products, which have longer life cycles, lends itself to traditional buyout models," he says.

That's not to say the high-tech industry has become as predictable as the steel, paper, and cotton industries. Any technology company, no matter what the product or market, is vulnerable to a slowdown, so it's inevitable that someday an LBO firm will make a big mistake.

"High tech is different from any other industry, and [LBO firms] haven't invested in the high end of high tech," says Deloitte's Baer. "But at some point, something will happen and [an LBO firm] could be screwed. If you have debt payments to make, you could be less patient with volatility."

Source: Jim Evans, "Leveraged Buyout Firms Go Tech," Upside magazine, October 1996.

Managing Your Business with Technology

Management has been an art for quite a long time. The best managers often have an innate ability to recruit, retain, and get the most out of great people over sustained periods of time. A healthy organization only makes this job a bit easier. Nevertheless, managers have been using tools and techniques (technologies if you will) to help them manage their companies since the Industrial Revolution. The genesis of using sophisticated technology as a framework for managerial decision making probably starts with Frederick Taylor using time and motion studies to figure out the best way to execute work in a factory. By today's standards, Taylor's time and motion studies would not be considered a technological advancement, nor would Ford's assembly-line production methods. However, these technologies revolutionized the way managers looked at and managed the work of the people in their employ.

Today, technology plays a critical role in *how managers run the corporation*. The role that technology plays varies depending on the company's point of view on how to use technology. Although there is not a clear delineation in how companies use technology, there are generally three major groupings that explain companies' behavior in this area:

- Companies that use technology to manage operations: Some companies use technology only to help manage the business via financial systems, project management tools, and production control.

- Companies that use technology to enable critical business processes: Other companies use technology to streamline processes, to reduce costs, and to improve cycle times. Examples of this are manufacturing control systems and enterprise resource planning.

- Companies that use technology to gain competitive advantage: The last group of companies use technology to gain advantage in the marketplace. Internet technologies that allow customers to interface with the company, as well as company-to-company electronic communications, fall into this category.

Keeping these broad classifications in mind, this chapter explores the following areas:

- Some of the technologies that are currently important in running a business today

- A whole host of specific uses of technology at both the industry and company level

- How leading companies use and manage technology

TECHNOLOGY EXISTED BEFORE COMPUTERS THAT HELPED MANAGERS RUN THEIR BUSINESSES

Managers have used technology for decision support for quite a long time. Arguably, management science was created by Frederick Taylor. Taylor's time and motion studies were, at the time, a technological breakthrough for how to improve productivity. This technology was improved on over the years by the quality management gurus such as Walter Shewart and Edwards Deming. The introduction of statistical process control techniques to monitor and improve factory performance is well documented. With the addition of computer technologies, it became much easier to collect and process information for management decision making. Thus, it is erroneous to think of technology merely as a bunch of computers handling accounts payable and the like. Instead, technology includes all scientific techniques and processes for improving work.

DANGER! The use of IT as a decision support tool should be complementary to good management practice, not a substitution. Ultimately, if people are not motivated and do not respond well to the company's operations, all the techniques in the world will not help the organization.

KEY CONCEPT **GAIN COMPETITIVE ADVANTAGE**

To be an effective user of technology, it is important to understand how technological advances and the relevant terminology evolved. Not too many years ago, all computing was done by a select few that knew how to make the large monolithic mainframe computer work. Businesspeople were merely users of the computer systems. And, in fact, most businesspeople only used output created by these large applications in the form of reports. Then, along came the PC. Although the first PCs were hardly usable for the average person, it was not long before the computing power that was once restricted to run only the most powerful applications became available to a far greater number of people. Computing power alone, though, albeit closer to the user, did not change the paradigm.

Two fundamental changes have occurred. First, when Microsoft introduced the first radical enhancement to the Windows-operating environment in the early 1990s, combined with equally explosive power increases in silicon put into PCs, an explosion of innovation began to occur for desktop computing. Whereas almost ten years before the spreadsheet was invented and put to use and the Apple Macintosh had its loyal fans, the openness of this new environment created a whole new bunch of computer programmers and entrepreneurs trying to make a buck. Countless new applications were created, from word processors to label makers to desktop database management systems. Suddenly, the PC became a general business tool.

The second fundamental change occurred in the user community of these new devices. It would not be much of an exaggeration to say that ten years ago most of the workforce had computerphobia. These strange devices were either used grudgingly, or not at all, by both long-time employees and even the younger workforce. This has clearly changed. Business has seen an influx of young professionals who have grown up on computers and electronic games (and I'm not talking about *Pong*). This has created a whole new computer-literate user community. At the same time, like with most new things, even the traditional employee has adapted and now largely accepts (and even sometimes flourishes) with the role of the computer in the workplace (Figure 2.1).

So, we now have a plethora of powerful technologies on a desktop, as well as a far more willing and educated user community. What does that leave us with? In many companies, the end users are doing as much or more computing than the information systems departments. They are building spreadsheets to analyze financial performance, database systems to organize information the way they like to see it, tracking systems for their smaller workgroups, and so on. In addition, these end users are making new demands on the information systems department and are educated on the latest trends in enterprise-wide computing. This shift has made it necessary for you, as a manager of these computer warriors and of critical business functions, to understand more and more about the technology business. By definition then, an ignorance of all computer jargon cannot simply be ignored. It is important to understand this terminology, not only because the business will spend a lot of money on these new systems, but also to ensure that your now computer-savvy workforce is getting all the tools needed to make the business successful.

Timeline	Dominant Computing Model
1970s to mid/late 1980s	Centralized computing
Mid/late 1980s to mid 1990s	Distributed computing
Late 1990s and beyond	End-user computing

FIGURE 2.1

TECHNOLOGY IS AN ENABLER AND IS USED THROUGHOUT THE ORGANIZATION IN EACH OF ITS CORE OPERATIONS

The Financial Services Industry Is Fueled by Technology

Companies in the financial services industry are enormous consumers of technology. In many ways, the technology is the business. Traders use information systems to price deals, analyze markets, and execute trades. In this case, from a management perspective, technology is a sine qua non for doing business. It is in this business that technology is at the forefront of how a corporation makes money.

This truism even extends to the market exchanges. Without computerized trade matching, the number of trades executed per day would be many less. Technology in this industry has created an engine for corporate liquidity and a worldwide economy. Although many financial firms strive to use technology to gain competitive advantage, the harsh reality is that, in many cases, it is merely a necessary cost (albeit large one) of doing business.

Point-of-Sale Technology Greatly Enhances Supply Chain Management

Along with the idea of statistical process control (SPC) is the more sophisticated technique of *production* or *manufacturing control.* Technology has become critical in managing the supply chain of many businesses. This notion is a rather simple one—information from a person in the supply chain drives the production schedules for a factory or other producer.

We often think of the idea that a business gets a batch of orders and then starts filling them. Because this is an overly simplistic model that leads to long lead times, we know that producers will rely, instead, on forecasts to figure out how much product they should make. The problem here is that the forecasts are often unreliable or out-and-out wrong, leading either to shortfalls or surplus or, at least, the timing is all screwed up, causing long lead times once again. So, how can technology help?

Meta Group Markets Independent IT Advice

Hal Kellman

If you think you have problems keeping up with the latest technology trends, how would you like to be the head of a Fortune 500 business unit?

Today, IT decisions involve evaluating new and rapidly evolving companies and products from multiple client-server vendors, as well as the interoperability of these products with one another and the existing legacy systems.

Today's lean and mean organizations do not have the internal resources to make the proper IT choices; they have to go outside for help. But where can you get strategic and tactical advice in planning, selecting, and implementing IT?

If you're inclined to listen to the software or hardware vendors, I've got a bridge that you can buy real cheap. Large professional service firms typically promote solutions that require their services on a continuing basis. There is a vital need for vendor-neutral, user-focused, broad-based IT market research coupled with personalized advice tailored to an organization's business environment and IT requirements. This is where Meta Group, Inc. comes in.

Meta Group, a leading independent market-assessment company, researches and analyzes developments and trends in computer hardware, software, communications, and related IT industries. Clients use Meta Group's services to develop cost-effective strategies for product positioning, marketing, and internal IT decision making. Specifically, clients can subscribe to any or all of ten different segments of Meta Group's research services (continuous services), each of which is focused on a specific subset of the IT industry. Key elements of Meta Group's business strategy include:

Expand client base. Meta Group's customers are substantial commercial and government users of IT. The company is expanding its product offerings, sales network, and marketing efforts.

Increase penetration of existing clients and maintain high retention rates. Meta Group is increasingly cross market-

(Continued)

(Continued)

ing its services, emphasizing improving its 80 percent yearly client retention.

Provide client-specific advice and emphasize client-analyst interaction. To provide a high level of personal service and client-analyst interaction, Meta Group maintains a client-analyst ratio of no higher than 50-to-1.

Leverage broad research coverage. The first vertical market offering, Healthcare Information Technology Strategies, was released in June 1995. Specific functional departments, such as sales and human resources, have been targeted with products tailored to their requirements.

Expand international markets. Meta Group uses 17 independent sales representative organizations globally and intends to substantially increase the number of its own research analysts based overseas.

Examples of continuous services offered to clients are:

Application development strategies. This service analyzes business application development strategies, including staff effectiveness and the uses of advanced software packages. Specific areas include computer architectures, object-oriented programming, client-server application initiatives, data warehouse applications, and organizational issues.

Services and system management strategies. This service focuses on management issues involved in three areas of shared computing infrastructure: network system management, customer support center, and managing third-party vendors and outsourcing agencies. The IT areas covered are enterprise systems management, help-desk reengineering, outsourcing and shared computing infrastructure.

The list price for continuous services ranges from $20,000 to $25,000 and is subject to discounts, including the number of different services subscribed to by a client. The average selling price is $14,000. As of June 30, nearly 1,000 client organizations had subscribed to 2,490 total services. Clients include 8 of the top ten Fortune 500 companies and 23 percent of the total Fortune 500.

Headquarters:	Stamford, Conn.
CEO:	Dale Kutnick
Employees:	175

(Continued)

(Continued)

Exchange/Symbol:	Nasdaq/METG
Shares outstanding:	8 million
52-week range*:	$20.50–$33.25
Market valuation*:	$184 million

Meta Group's principal direct competitor is the Gartner Group. Indirect competition comes from information providers, including electronic- and print-media companies and consulting firms.

Revenues in calendar 1992 were $8.5 million, resulting in a loss of $700,000. By 1995, revenues had exploded to $29.6 million, resulting in a profit of $1.2 million. Projected revenue for 1996 is $40 million to $42 million, with earnings of $3 million to $3.5 million; estimates for 1997 are revenues of $57 million to $59 million with earnings of $5.3 million to $5.8 million.

*$23.06/share (9/11/96).

Source: Hal Kellman, "Meta Group Markets Independent IT advice," Upside magazine (November 1996).

Editor's Note: Revenues for the first three quarters of calendar 1997 were $36 million. Hal Kellman, an independent investment adviser, is a former columnist for Upside magazine.

Clearly, the best of all worlds would be to produce as things are needed. Computer programs have been designed to estimate how much of a given product is needed based on data that is coming from the users of the product. There are quite a few interesting case studies we can examine that illustrate how technologies are used to manage the supply chain.

To take a simple example of how such a system works, assume that Pampers diapers are a key product. If one store is forwarding data to a computer about the sales of Pampers, the system can be programmed to ensure that the store is always stocked with the correct amount. (The system is based on information such as historical data, discounts, and demographic information for the area.) Pampers will be delivered to the inventory required so that shortages (angering customers) and surpluses (wasting shelf and warehouse space, incurring greater inventory costs) are avoided.

RUNNING THE OPERATION—USE A CENTRALIZED HELP DESK TO BETTER MANAGE YOUR TECHNOLOGY INVESTMENT

For the businessperson, the thought of a total cost of ownership for a personal computer sitting on a person's desktop at around $45,000 is mind numbing. Although there are other estimates that are less staggering, this is the quote from IT and management pundits at the Gartner Group; although the exact figure may be debatable, managers should realize the problem by now. The company is not merely paying for the cost of the computer, they are paying for the people paid to run it, namely the IT staff.

In addition, the company must absorb costs related to the time spent by end users (i.e., businesspeople) installing, configuring, troubleshooting, and asking their neighbors in the office how a piece of software works. I think a quick patrol around the office will reveal that much time is spent this way, both with internally developed applications, as well as with off-the-shelf software. So, how can time and money costs be minimized?

The use and promotion of a help desk run or outsourced by the IT group will help ease this problem. A help desk is the technology shop's equivalent to a customer service center. It is staffed by centrally located people assigned to answer the telephone regarding computer problems that the users are having. This type of department helps answer both simple questions about how to use software or debug problems, as well as more complicated computer snafus.

For managers, the help desk provides several areas of decision support. Using software that is specially built for help desk organizations, information such as the number of calls, the problem areas, and their resolutions can be captured. This information will help to adequately resource the technology department, identify training needs within the business, illustrate what software is particularly troublesome, and capture accurate estimates about the cost of particular software or hardware platforms.

Setting up a help desk is trivial. Making it work is not. There are many companies offering to provide help desk services, often in remote parts of the land where labor costs are cheaper. You frequently get what you pay for, so be careful. Ensure that vendors agree to service levels (e.g., for wait time and percent of questions answered). At the same time, make sure that you can measure how they are doing.

ADDITIONAL READING ON HELP DESKS

Corporation Microsoft, *Microsoft Sourcebook for the Help Desk* (includes book and CD-ROM: "Techniques and Tools for Support Organization Design and Management"). 2d ed. Microsoft Press, 1997. Paperback, 400 pages.

Thomas, Andrew H., and Robert M. Steele. *The Virtual Help Desk: Strategic Management Center.* Intl Thomson Computer Press, 1996. Paperback, 200 pages.

RUNNING THE OPERATION—USE TOOLS TO HELP PLAN AND MANAGE PROJECTS

Tools support the effective management of projects. Most of the tools mentioned hereafter are now available in software form, such as Microsoft's Project. Although there are numerous tools to assist the project manager, three merit discussion here due to their utility and prevalent use. The description of these tools was adapted from the Web site for the Information Policy Office of the State of Minnesota. In researching this topic, this policy statement by the State of Minnesota included all of the appropriate tools and concepts required to build a good plan.

Milestones

Milestone-planning techniques allow projects to evolve as they move through the development process. This technique does not attempt to fully predict all project requirements and problems in advance. Rather, the project is allowed to progress at its own rate.

Stellar Performer: Wal-Mart

Wal-Mart is known as a discount department store and as the quintessential American success company. When we think of Wal-Mart, we think of doing business simply, to capture the consumer through value and consistency. Behind the scenes, Wal-Mart relies on fairly sophisticated technologies to ensure that it keeps its suppliers in the loop with sales of product.

Each Wal-Mart store is equipped with systems that communicate via satellite to a central Wal-Mart computer that keeps track of sales of all the Wal-Mart stores. Based on this information, Wal-Mart can quickly forward information to key suppliers about how sales of their product are doing, allowing for replenished inventories, as well as the best prices for Wal-Mart.

Stellar Performer:
Mrs. Fields Cookies

Those luscious cookies that you buy at the mall from Mrs. Fields are not merely cooked up according to whatever the person working believes is the correct batch or based on some stale data from company headquarters. Instead, each store forwards sales data on a daily basis to headquarters computers. This data is used to figure out how much of a particular cookie should be made the next day. The central computer then downloads the information to the store in the computer to map out how much of each type should be made so that Mrs. Fields is consistently meeting the needs of the customers. At the same time, this information can be used by the Mrs. Fields franchise to ensure that product lines are meeting the projected sales goals and to carefully track new product introductions.

Fast Forward to the Real World

Interview with Jeff Bezos of Amazon.com

Karen Southwick

Building a successful retail business on the Internet has so far proved to be an elusive goal, but Amazon.com, though not profitable, is as close as anyone. From 1992 to 1994, Jeff Bezos was like one of the Wall Street wunderkinds whom Tom Wolfe parodied in *Bonfire of the Vanities.* Still in his 20s, Bezos helped build a complex hedge fund at D.E. Shaw & Co. Then he caught the Internet bug, moved his family to Seattle, and operated his start-up out of the proverbial garage. His passion was to exploit the Web's potential for electronic retailing, and Bezos picked books as the product most likely to sell successfully on-line. Now 32 years old, Bezos is the head of Amazon.com, housed in a converted warehouse in Seattle's seedy south-of-the-dome (Sodo) neighborhood. The company today employs about 70 people and recently received its first venture capital infusion from Kleiner Perkins Caufield & Byers of Menlo Park, California. Bezos runs his company in a lean-and-mean fashion, using makeshift desks and a clutch of 20-something workers primed by stock options and the vision of someday being part of a billion-dollar enterprise.

UPSIDE: **Why did you decide to leave Wall Street and start this company?** BEZOS: Two years ago nobody knew how many people were on the World Wide Web, but what was noticed was that Web usage was growing at 2,300 percent a year. The interesting thing about anything that grows with that speed is, yesterday it's invisible and tomorrow it's everywhere. I started thinking about what kinds of opportunities are there going to be in this new Web space. It was clear that the Web technology, even though it was rudimentary, would support primitive interactive retailing. I thought that the content areas were going to be very crowded, and it wasn't clear what the revenue model was to make money off of content, so transaction-based business made sense to me. And it seemed to me that vertical industry groups were a good place to start if you could pick one that really made sense in terms of the technology. So I made a list of 20 different product areas and chose books as the first batch of product to sell on the Web.

(Continued)

(Continued)

How did you happen to pick books? There's so much you could sell on the Web. Books have a very unusual characteristic; there are so many different books. That's totally different from any other product category. The number two product category is music. There are about 200,000 active music CDs in print at any given time. There are 1.5 million English-language books in print at any given time. If you take all languages worldwide, it's about 3 million books active and in print. So when you're talking about a large number of titles like that, that's where computers really start to shine because of their sorting and organizing capabilities. There's no way to have a physical bookstore with 1.1 million titles, which we have on our site. No metropolitan area is large enough to economically support such a store. There's no way to have a printed paper catalog like that, either. Our catalog, if you were to print it, would be the size of seven New York City phone books.

Right now Web technology is still rudimentary enough that the value proposition you offer to your customer has to be extremely large if you're going to make them put up with the sort of inconvenience of doing business on the Web. Your modem line hangs up on you, your call-waiting clicks in and everything gets messed up. These are the kinds of things that happen every day on the Web, and basically the value proposition has to be so strong that, effectively, you can only do things on the Web that you cannot do any other way, and that's why books are the best product.

But shopping itself is as much a social experience as it is buying something. Absolutely. People do go to bookstores to have a good time; they drink coffee and they mingle. That's why people always ask me, "So, is Amazon.com going to put bookstores out of business?" And that does not make sense. It's analogous to asking, "Did TV put the movies out of business?" Of course not. In fact, Hollywood is a bigger industry now than it ever was before the invention of television. And it's the same thing here. We won't be able to do the same types of things as great physical bookstores, which have good sofas, good lattes and all this stuff. And even little things they have that we can't do, like I love to open the book and hear the bindings creak. We're not going to compete along those dimensions. But there are some aspects we do that you could never do in a physical bookstore that are also fun and engaging. A lot of those revolve around customer-to-customer interaction and customer-to-author interaction.

(Continued)

(Continued)

Anybody can come into our store and post a review on any of the 1.1 million books, and that review is permanently associated with that book's entry in our catalog. And that's something you couldn't do in a physical bookstore. Another example is, we let authors come into our site and self-administer interviews. They click on this [icon] and basically a Web page comes up that asks a bunch of stock interview questions. Authors can just type answers into the Web form and it becomes a live interview on our site associated with all that author's books. Authors can also leave their e-mail addresses, so our customers can e-mail authors and say, "I love your book," "I hated your book" or whatever.

Another thing is that anybody who has their own Web site can set up their own [specialized] bookstore. Let's say you're the world's expert on dinosaurs and you are the Webmaster of the dinosaur Web site. You can pick the 10 best dinosaur books, list them on your site and provide some editorial context, and then link from your site directly into our catalog. When your dinosaur Web browsers come to the dinosaur Web site, they can buy those books from us and we can track the sales generated that way and pay you a commission.

I also notice you allow interaction between readers themselves, so I can come on and say, "I really loved this last book and I would recommend it." You can come on our Web site and post that message, and then anybody who looks up that book can see it. And we give you the option of leaving your e-mail address alongside that posting, so you can say, "I loved this book on [this subject] and does anybody out there know of any other great books on it?"

So why the name Amazon.com? What does it mean? Earth's biggest river, Earth's biggest bookstore. The Amazon River is 10 times as large as the next largest river, which is the Mississippi, in terms of volume of water. Twenty percent of the world's fresh water is in the Amazon River Basin, and we have six times as many titles as the world's largest physical bookstore.

I guess the idea is that eventually you will sell other products besides books. Perhaps. It's very hard to do even one thing in a truly excellent way. Trying to do two things in a truly excellent way can get very tricky.

(Continued)

(Continued)

You mentioned once that music was a possibility. Music is a possibility, but there are going to be a lot of people out there focused on music, and doing a really great job. We may get involved in that at some point in the future, but right now we're very focused on books.

What about your pricing? You have discounts, but you also charge a transaction fee. We charge a shipping charge. We are actually the broadest discounters in the world. We discount 300,000 titles, which is twice as many titles as the largest physical bookstore even carries; we discount those books anywhere between 10 and 30 percent. The other 750,000 titles in our catalog we sell at list price.

What is your revenue model? Is it just based on the transaction itself? Currently, it's purely transactional.

It does seem to me there would be opportunities for advertising. Any of the big book publishers or authors themselves could advertise. Have you looked at that at all? Or is there an ethical problem? We know that there's demand for it. We get requests all the time. So far we just haven't done any of it, but it certainly makes a lot of sense. I don't think there's any ethical issues here, as long as it's clearly advertisement and not editorial. It's strictly a resource constraint problem. As we prioritize, we'll eventually get to it.

When do you expect profitability? Have you changed from your two-year prediction? It hasn't really changed. It's strictly a function of our business plan and our revenue.

So '97, '98 would be reasonable? When we were founding the company two years ago, I told [our investors] not to expect profits for five years. We've exceeded all of our expectations, but we've also made our business plan more aggressive. It's a moving target. We're not focused on trying to make the company profitable. If we're profitable anytime in the short term it'll just be an accident.

When do you think the Web is going to become an important venue for retailing? People are projecting that over the next four years you'll see something like 8 percent of retail sales done on-line.

(Continued)

(Continued)

And you're forecasting that some day Amazon's going to be a $1 billion company. Any timetable on that? In the year 2000, our goal is to be one of the world's leading bookstores. Since the world's leading bookstores are billion-dollar companies, people impute that.

What's to prevent somebody like a Barnes and Noble or a Borders from opening up a site like this on the Web? With their name recognition, wouldn't that be a significant threat to you? I think it does make sense for them to do that and I think they will do that. But their brand names work for them and against them. They work for them because they're well-known, well-established brand names. They work against them because they already occupy a particular slot in the consumer's mind, which is that of a physical bookstore. We're going to position ourselves as the on-line bookstore, and that's a very important branding distinction and something they can't do. The other thing is that we have a significant head start and we're going to make that gap widen, not narrow. But we expect to face competition.

Who do you see as your competition today? We're by far the largest bookseller out there in terms of the number of titles we offer for sale and the services we provide. We are, for all intents and purposes, competing against a vacuum right now. That's not going to last.

You can already start to tell some things about the customers by what they buy. Do you then make further suggestions based on their past preferences? One thing that interactive retailing holds for the future is that you can redecorate the store for every customer. Right now we're not doing anything with that type of thing. But it would certainly make sense to me that if we know that every time you come to the store you buy science fiction, we should redecorate the store and show you the latest science fiction. Right now if you go into a physical bookstore, they have to put in the front the *New York Times* best sellers. They have to put the thing that everybody buys.

The lowest common denominator. That doesn't have to be true on-line. We have two services now that customers can sign up for. One is called "Eyes" and it's our personal notification service, where you can come in and register your interest. You can say, "I want to

(Continued)

(Continued)

know every time John Grisham publishes a new book," or "Please notify me about every new book on kayaking or every book on sea kayaking." We can do that. It's totally automated, and because the marginal cost to us of sending an e-mail message is so low, we can afford to offer that service without charging for it.

And then there's our editor's service. That is not a fully automated service. That's a human-generated service. In each of our major genres and categories, like science fiction, computer books and so on, we have a freelance editor who will actually send e-mail updates saying, Here's the latest, greatest things I've been reading in the historical fiction genre or whatever.

Maybe one of the things that we can do is when you come in and if you search for books on kayaks, we'll show you the list of 225 books we have on kayaks, but we'll also show you an advertisement for a company that sells kayaks. And you can click on that and go to their Web site and buy a kayak. So I do think there are a lot of ways we could start to help put people together with the products they want.

But you're not selling your customers' names. No, we're not. We don't have any plans to do that. We have an Amazon.com Bill of Rights, and it specifically lays out what we don't do with preference data. It gives people a way to completely opt out of ever having their data used in any way.

How many people have you actually had buy from you at this point? It's tens of thousands of people. I can't tell you more than that. You know, Bill Gates is a customer of ours. We didn't actually even know that until he was interviewed by *PC Week,* and *PC Week* said to Bill Gates, "So how 'bout Internet commerce?" And Bill Gates said, "Well, I buy my all my books at Amazon.com."

Great endorsement. I know, and he proceeded to lay out our marketing proposition, which is, "I do it because I'm very busy, I don't have much time. They've got a big selection, and they've been very reliable." That's exactly what we want to convey. The only thing he didn't include is: We also have great prices. But it probably doesn't matter to him.

Source: Karen Southwick, "Interview with Jeff Bezos of Amazon.com," Upside magazine (October 1996).

Editor's Note: Since this interview was conducted, Barnes & Noble has started its own on-line bookstore and is engaged in heated competition with Amazon.com that's spurring heavy discounting by both. Amazon.com also completed a successful public offering in 1997, but it had yet to reach profitability. For the first three quarters of 1997, the company lost $18 million on revenue of $82 million. Karen Southwick, formerly executive editor of Upside magazine, is now editor of Upside Books.

This type of tool is best used for projects that are not easily predictable or straightforward. A major benefit of the milestone tool is its simplicity. Milestone planning involves establishing predetermined, significant checkpoints, whereby management can determine whether further commitment of resources to the project is warranted. Checkpoints can be based either on time, cost, or deliverables. For example, checkpoints can be set at three-month intervals, at which time assessments will be performed to reconfirm the project. Furthermore, milestones can be considered kind of lines in the sand for management to assess the health (or lack of it) for a project.

Gantt Charts

Gantt charts are another common tool used to manage projects and are among the most popular project management software tools. Gantt charts are best used when projects are somewhat predictable and straightforward. Gantt charts provide graphical representation of project tasks, progress, and deadlines. Gantt charts provide a description of tasks to be performed along with their start and completion dates.

Gantt charts can be broken down into further levels of detail. For example, an item on a high-level Gantt chart might be gathering of business requirements. Another Gantt chart can be created that breaks gathering of business requirements into more detailed tasks, such as meeting with project sponsors or understanding existing computer system features.

PERT Charts

PERT charts are another common project management tool. PERT charts are best used when the project is predictable and straightforward, because they try to depict dependencies among project tasks. In addition, they graphically represent the sequence of tasks required to complete a project.

The PERT chart directly establishes relationships and sequential dependencies among project tasks. The total time to complete a project can be determined by locating the longest path in the chart—the critical path. When the critical path is clearly identified, it is much easier to determine the repercussions of not completing tasks on a timely basis. When a task on the critical path is not completed, the overall project schedule will be impacted accordingly.

Typically, a PERT chart is created along with a corresponding project table that defines responsible personnel, estimated times, actual times, estimated costs, and actual costs. Using this information, project management can monitor and control project performance.

RUNNING THE OPERATION—SPREADSHEETS ARE STILL THE MOST IMPORTANT PC APPLICATION

It would be a crime to write anything down about decision support tools in a management setting without mentioning spreadsheets. Spreadsheets were invented in the early 1980s and became the first killer application for the PC. The ability to do complex financial, statistical, and other numerical analyses at a single desktop was, and continues to be, a great advancement. Without spreadsheets, management approaches like open-book management, financial literacy, and benchmarking would be impossible.

Businesspeople unfamiliar with the spreadsheet should really learn how to use one. This may be the single easiest way to capture and analyze financial information such as budget and sales projections.

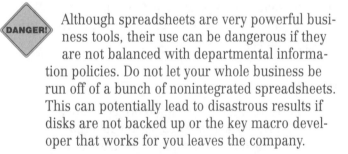

Although spreadsheets are very powerful business tools, their use can be dangerous if they are not balanced with departmental information policies. Do not let your whole business be run off of a bunch of nonintegrated spreadsheets. This can potentially lead to disastrous results if disks are not backed up or the key macro developer that works for you leaves the company.

USING SPREADSHEETS TO PREDICT AND EVALUATE IT INVESTMENT

One practical use of spreadsheets is to help a manager weigh the value and urgency of any project. Its leftmost column would list the projects your internal customers have asked for. Across the top of the spreadsheet, column headings might indicate considerations and constraints that come to mind when you think about the projects. As your company's decision maker, you fill the resulting cells with numbers, indicating each project's strengths and weaknesses in relation to those parameters.

If you have the final word on which projects will be addressed first, last, or never, the spreadsheet can help you explain your decision to those who made the requests. If your job is to advise a board or committee, the spreadsheet can help them understand your recommendations.

Brian Wegner, vice president of health information systems at Fortis, Inc., an insurance company in Milwaukee, uses spreadsheets to analyze and justify IT projects. Wegner's system has simplified decision making in a complex organization. He has reorganized the way IT investment decisions are made, complete with a repeatable, numeric way of assigning priorities. Using his spreadsheet model, Wegner can arrange project requests in numerical order of importance and predict which are more or less likely to be approved. "Having a formal process improves communications and ensures that we're working on the right things," Wegner says. At present, he's using the spreadsheet model for a pilot program in application development for Fortis. Eventually, Wegner says, it will be extended to the rest of the enterprise.[1]

USING RESEARCH AND DEVELOPMENT TO CREATE NEW PRODUCTS AND FIND NEW MARKETS

Research and development (R&D) is the starting point for much of the product innovation that we have enjoyed as citizens and workers. Without active research laboratories at places such as AT&T, IBM, and Xerox, activities such as speaking on the telephone or simply photocopying, which we all take for granted, probably would not have advanced as far or as fast as they have. In recent times, R&D has taken on a whole new meaning for companies, in particular, those in the cutting-edge technology category.

Within the last five years, we have certainly lived in the age of innovation. Spawned by rapid advancements in computer microprocessors by a company such as Intel, computer hardware, software, and communications gear companies are in a constant game of trying to leapfrog one another or, at a minimum, trying to find niches to reach new heights of profitability. This advancement is being driven by some tried-and-true mogul-like entrepreneurs, like Bill Gates at Microsoft, as well as the loads of venture capital–bankrolled technology start-ups in Silicon Valley, all dreaming of the IPO success of companies like Netscape.

Clearly, almost all companies need to innovate their products to remain competitive. This is equally true for the single-person service company to the largest of multinationals. Of course, the strategy for staying innovative differs widely from industry to industry. The point of this section is not to tell you how to innovate your product lines; instead, the focus is on how to learn from some of the cutting-edge technology leaders in their approach to R&D. In particular, the manner by which leading companies and Wall Street darlings, such as Intel and Microsoft, manage R&D will provide insight on how to manage some of your leading technology investments.

Stellar Performer: Intel

Intel Corporation is the industry leader for producing the micro-processor that has fueled the exponential growth of power for the PC. Arguably, the rapid evolution of the Intel x86 architecture has created the wealth for companies such as Microsoft, Lotus, and other PC software vendors (See Figure 2.2). This growth has been equally important to the PC manufacturers, such as Compaq and Dell, that are able to sell new computers on a consistent basis due to the need for more power at the desktop. Intel's commitment to R&D is key in their corporate values. A blurb found on the Intel home page sum-marizes their strategy toward R&D.

"We at Intel have long known that our growth depends on the continued expansion of the PC platform's capabilities. The more users demand of PCs, the more power will be required to drive them, and the more microprocessors will be sold. In response, we have expanded Intel's role in the computing industry over the last several years. Act-ing as a sort of R&D lab and strategic think tank to the industry, we work with PC makers, software developers, and PC users to under-stand their future needs and wishes, and work intensely with industry leaders to develop products or specifications that meet those needs."

Extrapolating on this quotation, it is quite easy to understand how Intel uses its R&D capabilities to create strategic advantage. They do this by:

- Creating a symbiotic relationship between Intel and software pro-ducers—the need and desire to do more with software on the computer pushes Intel to design chips that will be faster and that will accommodate the type of business needs that the developers who are close to end users need.

- Creating a symbiotic relationship between Intel and hardware manufacturers—the software has to run somewhere, so Intel needs to ensure that the hardware manufacturers are successful. Their components must be easy to work with and resilient. A clear example of this strategy is the push to make chips less susceptible to heat problems, so that they can run effectively in smaller and smaller computers.

- Working with end customers on special needs—Intel has been successful in creating products for video teleconferencing by lis-tening to customers, as well as trying to develop specialized chip solutions to solve problems such as floating point performance to ensure that they will gain critical enterprise presence.

Notice that Intel's strategy is focused around customers and others in its stream of commerce. Intel does not merely adopt a

(Continued)

(Continued)

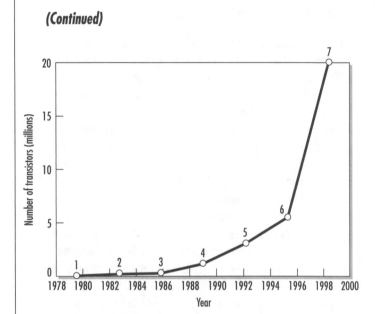

FIGURE 2.2 *The numbers on the graph, 1 through 7, represent the following:*

1. *8088—29,000 transistors June 1979*
2. *80286—134,000 transistors February 1982*
3. *Intel 386—275,000 transistors October 1985*
4. *Intel 486—1,200,000 transistors April 1989*
5. *Pentium—3,100,000 transistors March 1993*
6. *Pentium Pro—5,500,000 transistors November 1995*
7. *Merced—20,000,000+ transistors 1999*

Source: Upside *magazine (December 1997).*

build-it-and-they-will-come attitude. Instead, they are extremely focused on those that they will ultimately depend on. All nontechnology companies have similar requirements in which their products are only successful if others in the supply chain work with them. Therefore, in terms of R&D, Intel believes that money spent on being connected with customers and suppliers will ease and speed relationships. So, spending money on building technology solutions in which companies can share information is valuable. This is both a business need and a heavy-duty technical application due to communications and information security issues.

Source: www.intel.com.

Stellar Performer: Microsoft

The dominant software company in the world fuels much of its success from a rich approach to R&D and spends an enormous amount of money on R&D. Microsoft's R&D expenditures in 1995 were $860 million. In fact, 6,884 employees of over 19,500 are labeled as members of R&D staff. With over one-third of a workforce looking at innovation, it is no wonder that Microsoft is always close to a product in any burgeoning market.

Microsoft's strategy is to invest an enormous amount of money in pushing the technologies it has made when it is deemed appropriate. They have a very sophisticated product-release strategy that supports its efforts in R&D, product design, and market research. Simply put, Microsoft's approach is likened to a hedging strategy. They invest in everything from interactive TV to intelligent homes. This strategy has been extremely effective when it comes to ensuring that Microsoft does not miss a market opportunity. For instance, when it seemed that Microsoft executives got caught missing the Internet ball several years ago, why were they able to react so decisively to remedy the situation? It was not as if they had not looked into these technologies or thought about them; instead, it was just an increased focus on something that they already had spent quite a bit of time and money on.

Source: Microsoft Web page.

From the Field
The Internet Creates New Markets: On-Line Ticketing

According to Forrester Research, the on-line ticket market will top $10 billion by 2001. Until the Internet emerged on the scene just a few short years ago, there was virtually no market for on-line ticketing. Although the Web has not been a panacea for most businesses, many consumers are very comfortable purchasing airline, sporting event, and concert tickets over this media, because it is not the type of thing that the consumer needs to touch to feel comfortable.

Consumer comfort has created new markets for companies such as Preview Travel, which started as a producer of travel-related television programs. Within ten months of launching a Web-based ticketing business, Preview Travel has propelled itself into the top 50 travel agencies in terms of revenue.

A more established ticketing agency, Ticketmaster, also uses the Internet to touch customers. Ticketmaster offers customers the added value of purchasing tickets electronically. In addition, and perhaps just as important, Ticketmaster has added merchandising and branding opportunities via the same mechanism. The sale of a ticket can come with the sale of a T-shirt for the concert or a hat for the ball game.

This paradigm will probably expand to the idea of E-tickets, in which physical delivery of a ticket will no longer be necessary at all. Consumers will merely need to show proper identification to gain entry to an event or onto an airplane.

Source: Information Week *(1 September 1997).*

Facing Reality in the Virtual Factory

Kathleen A. Henning

Imagine a world in which your business exists in both the physical and the computer world. Imagine being able to adjust capacity, introduce new products, change product mix/volumes, modify layouts, alter inventory policies, revise procedures, and test various production scenarios on the computer-based facility before modifying your physical operations and without production disruption. Imagine that when you make these changes, the computer brings an animated facility to life and runs the proposed operations so you can verify that new ideas and programs will meet your business objectives before spending a cent. You can approach each working day with confidence, because you tested your finite production schedule in advance. Your continuous improvement teams can use the computer-based factory to productively understand and improve operations across functional and operational boundaries. Imagine this world, and you have imagined simulation modeling—the interactive virtual factory that provides companies with the knowledge to effectively make the critical decisions required in today's uncertain business environment.

International economic conditions and business competition have prompted corporations to change their business strategies. To remain competitive, companies must improve their manufacturing, logistics, and management methods. Manufacturing is no longer just a means to produce a product. Manufacturing is a strategic weapon used by companies to allow them to produce high-quality parts at lower costs in record lead times. However, making these changes involves risk and often the outlay of large capital expenditures. Simulation provides a tool to allow manufacturers to better understand their options, guide them in design and operational improvements, substantially reduce investment and change-incurred risks, and ultimately improve business profits and performance.

Simulation is a tool for testing production, material handling, warehousing, distribution systems, and operational concepts before decisions, equipment, and systems are finalized. It provides a computer-based, dynamic, statistical representation of the actual systems and facility being modeled. Performing as the physical system

(Continued)

(Continued)

does, it allows the dynamics of manufacturing and logistics to be studied and understood in detail before any capital expenditures are made and without disrupting current production.

Today's simulation software provides two- or three-dimensional animation, in addition to the statistical output for decision making. It offers a check-and-balance system for managers, planners, engineers, and operators to visualize their planned changes in products, sales, equipment, layouts, polices, methods, labor, and automation. Cross-functional teams can use simulation to test their alternate improvement concepts quickly and effectively on a computer-based factory. Teams and/or individuals can then improve their solutions by interactively testing alternative ideas. This process allows for a greatly compressed continuous improvement cycle, because it brings people together, eliminates ineffective solutions before implementation, and leap frogs several smaller changes into a greatly improved, reduced-step, overall change process. Through its ability to be used in team-based environments, simulation also builds ownership and confidence across diverse disciplines and eliminates many of the people-based barriers to change. In other words, simulation allows you to:

1. Gather the known (or better-known) elements of your manufacturing operations, such as layout, equipment rates, process flow, equipment downtimes, labor work schedules, product mix, production-scheduling methods, system control logic, and manual and material-handling methods and rates.

2. Map these into a computer model.

3. Test-run proposed facility and operations concepts.

4. Evaluate the model based on important performance criteria, such as flexibility, cost, manufacturing lead time, inventory, labor requirements, line balancing, throughput, productivity, equipment quantities/usage, and bottleneck identification.

5. Try various what-if alternatives to determine the preferred concept in terms of performance and cost for your business or facility.

The Benefits and Applications of Simulation

Simulation can help manufacturers, distributors, and service industries improve their business positions through productively testing and improving their operations. Organizations that have asked the types of what-if questions below are candidates for simulation.

- What if we added a new production line? Do we really need the proposed equipment? Can we get by with our existing equipment?

(Continued)

(Continued)

- What if we reengineered the company? Will the reengineered environment truly allow us to reduce our lead times by the 60 percent required to match our competitor's lead times?

- What if we implemented a focused factory environment? Will the focused factory environment provide us with the flexibility that we need to meet our customers' ever-changing market demands?

- What if we added more people instead of, or in addition to, new equipment? Will adding people help or hurt our production output?

- What if we reallocated our tasks to different personnel? Will we be able to improve our output without sacrificing customer service?

Simulation helps companies answer the what-if questions that plague modernization efforts. Through simulation, companies get a bird's-eye view of future operations, providing them with a changeable tool to test their questions, alternatives, and/or concerns before finalizing their plans.

For example, imagine a food producer trying to determine the feasibility of a new product line. This company currently produces two types of pizza crusts and is considering augmenting its product line to include bagels. Simulation can help determine the quantity of needed new equipment and whether equipment can be shared between lines without sacrificing customer service, labor requirements, and costs. Using simulation, the company can review the effects of various production levels of both the current and proposed products before making the decision to move forward with the new bagel line.

Simulation allows businesses to make more informed decisions with greater confidence. Here are some examples of how simulation has been applied in a variety of settings:

Facility Sizing (Manufacturing and Warehouse)—At a gas turbine—manufacturing warehouse and spare parts distribution center, simulation identified the required receiving/shipping areas; floor storage; high-bay, large-parts storage; and miniload capacity for this facility. The simulation also identified opportunities for significantly decreasing facility size and lead times by making simple changes in handling and inspection procedures. This led to increased profitability and decreased capital and operational costs.

Facility and Equipment Layout—At a disk manufacturer, simulation tested alternate layouts and material-handling concepts. It also verified the capacity and flexibility requirements of the process equipment, material-handling devices, and layout.

(Continued)

(Continued)

Material-Handling Equipment Requirements, Control Specification, and Scheduling—At a tobacco-processing facility, simulation tested the manufacturer's receiving area concept to support a doubling of capacity within the manufacturing facility. The model identified over $2 million of capital equipment that could be eliminated without sacrificing support of throughput and response time needs.

Group Technology Manufacturing/Facility Design—At a power tools manufacturer, a simulation detailed both the current manufacturing environment and the proposed, focused factory environment to assess capacity requirements, lead times, throughput, and flow issues. The simulation helped identify areas in which group technology product family classifications fit or deviated from the production cell classifications for assessment of various manufacturing cell configurations.

Labor Requirements and Scheduling—At a test laboratory, simulation allowed improvement of task allocation and verification of the number of people required to support a quick-turnaround test operation for high-tech production. The test area included over 20 pieces of process equipment to be managed by approximately four operators in a mixture of clean-room and non-clean-room environments that required extensive gowning and degowning by operators migrating between areas and equipment. This simulation provided a preferred task allocation and priority schedule to minimize non-value-added time and improve lead times that ultimately reduced the storage time for production parts waiting to be shipped until test results were verified.

Computer-Integrated Manufacturing Design and Analysis—At a silicon production facility, simulation allowed the manufacturer to test its next-generation, highly automated facility to support future products and additional capacity requirements for current products. The new facility required high levels of mechanical and information systems automation because of clean-room requirements and increasing size and yield requirements of new products. The simulation determined the quantity of equipment required for each phase to meet market demands while improving cash flow. It also streamlined the overall design and provided a three-dimensional animated specification to enable the multiple material-handling and controls vendors to understand their individual requirements and interfaces with other systems. Through early team sessions and model validation improvement, the model also defined the opera-

(Continued)

(Continued)

tional concepts, control strategies, and scheduling logic required to support the make-to-order environment with minimum lead times, minimum storage, and maximum throughput. This simulation will also be used for finite capacity scheduling when the new facility goes on-line.

Just-in-Time/Lean Manufacturing Design and Analysis—A make-to-order electronics assembly manufacturer was experiencing tremendous sales increases but was tormented by downtimes caused by lack of material availability at the assembly lines at the right times. A simulation model was developed, and alternatives were tested, including assembly-line kanban quantities, kitting, equipment configuration, dock-to-floor concepts, and other operational concepts. Results significantly increased both throughput and flexibility.

Business Process Reengineering—At a time-share resort, a reengineering simulation provided data to support doubling the number of time-share units. The project reviewed and tested alternatives in materials management/purchasing, engineering, expediting, housekeeping operations scheduling, and maintenance management. The model identified and validated approximately $1 million in immediate annual savings, achievable through minimal cost changes in policies, scheduling, and materials management, and over $2 million in savings as the operations double in size.

Production Scheduling—In manufacturing and service industries, simulation-based finite scheduling provides verification and improvement of labor and equipment scheduling before schedules are released to operators. By running the proposed plan through the facility and reporting on-order completions, lead times, output, inventories, and usage, the simulation allows the planner to determine whether delivery deadlines will be met. The scheduler can then test alternate scheduling rules/techniques and change order priorities and resource allocations to improve the schedule before releasing it to the shop floor or work crews.

Strategic Planning—Although strategic planning in the United States rarely spans more than 5 years, it is not unusual to find 100-year plans in Japanese organizations. Because simulations are built as probabilistic, statistical models, they provide strong tools to look into the future with what-if analysis to understand and guide the company over the long term. In one such simulation, the organization modeled various R&D options, probabilities of resultant new products, time frames to achieve new products, and resource require-

(Continued)

(Continued)

ments/allocation techniques. The model focused on research and technical activities and the chances of maximizing successful new product output. Because of the accelerated run speed of the simulation, 100 years could be run in approximately one minute, so that numerous alternatives could be tested and compared. The model provided corporate leaders with a new approach to maximize new product introductions over the long run.

Theory of Constraints—At an automotive supplier plagued by unreliable processes, late orders, and inadequate materials management and handling procedures, the simulation modeled the existing operation, identifying the bottlenecks in equipment, policies, layout, and procedures. Concepts were then tested to improve capacity and uptime through the bottleneck operations, resulting in an over-50-percent improvement in throughput (and sales) without additional capital expenditures.

Simulation as a Full Life Cycle Tool

Simulation aids decision making throughout the complete life cycle of businesses, facilities, and products. It can be used in initial conception and planning, detailed design, construction and implementation, and regular production.

During initial conception, planners use simulation as a tool to test the feasibility of a wide range of business, facility, and operational concepts. The planning team—made up of representatives from research, marketing, engineering, production, materials, and distribution—can jointly observe the effects of interdepartmental concepts and programs, allowing decisions to be concentrated toward the good of the overall company.

Detailed design begins when corporate and project direction, scope, and initial concepts have been established. In this phase, ideas progress as designs are fully developed. Specifications are developed, layouts and staffing plans are finalized, and operating parameters are fine-tuned. By testing alternate vendor configurations, debugging vendor-specific considerations, and streamlining implementation, simulation tests the finer detail of design and operational concepts.

In the implementation phase, simulation can be used to train the operating team on the new operating environment. Animated videos of the simulation can be sent to vendors to allow them to better understand company expectations of equipment and the interfaces between their systems and other components.

(Continued)

(Continued)

When start-up has been completed and the operation slips into regular production, simulation is still a valuable business tool. It can be used for simulation-based scheduling, providing what-if finite capacity–scheduling analysis to verify that the plant will continue to meet order targets. Furthermore, operations never truly reach a steady state. Although the facility is in production, there are always new products and technologies that could be added. Simulation can test each change to ensure the feasibility of any modifications. Simulation should also continue to be part of the training program for new employees and be incorporated into continuing improvement teams so that employee suggestions can be tested.

Simulation helps businesses approach the future with confidence. By functioning as an interactive virtual factory, it offers a business insurance policy that allows companies to model their proposed facilities, layout, procedures, and equipment in the computer; test alternative scenarios; and verify performance parameters before committing capital and operating costs to a new or revised program. When used effectively, this virtual factory stimulates creativity and technical capability. It also helps companies improve operations efficiency, increase throughput, streamline lead times, decrease capital investment, improve flexibility, decrease inventories, reduce risks associated with change, and increase the profitability of the operations modeled. Organizations that have run simulation projects have reported such benefits as capital avoidance of over $2.4 million; a 50-percent throughput improvement without additional resources; operating savings of over $1 million; improved flexibility and responsiveness; and improved design and integration of people, equipment, procedures, layout, and systems. Of tremendous use in the design of new facilities and systems, the reengineering and modernization of existing operations, day-to-day improvement planning, and finite scheduling, simulation is a tool that enables companies to effectively make the critical decisions required in today's uncertain business environment.

Source: Kathleen A. Henning, "Facing Reality in the Virtual Factory," National Productivity Review, 15, No. 4: 7–14.

Editor's Note: Kathleen A. Henning is a partner at Synesis International, Inc., in Greenville, South Carolina, where she serves as the director of planning and operations engineering. She has provided operations performance improvement and systems integration–consulting and implementation services for such companies as Alfmeier, ALCOA, Coca-Cola, Cryovac, General Electric, General Foods, Motorola, Owens-Corning, Philip Morris, Verbatim, and Vistana Resorts. She is president of the Greenville-Spartanburg Chapter of the Institute of Industrial Engineers and is on the board of directors of the Industrial Crescent Chapter of the American Production and Inventory Control Society.

3

People and Technology

I
It is important for every businessperson to understand what it takes to make software and other
technology projects successful, which means that
they both work and are appropriate to the company's needs. It is also critical for managers to
understand how technology affects the worker. This
ranges broadly from how technology impacts each
employee's performance to how a company can
best integrate technology into internal processes.
This chapter covers five areas of discussion that
explain how people can manage the use and direction of their company's technology choices.

1. Roles and responsibilities of the businesspeople
   and complementary IT organizational roles
   (i.e., training, return on investment [ROI]).

2. How to recognize warning signs of technology
   project slips and cost overruns.

3. Issues related to managing computer people
   including the art versus the science of software
   development.

4. As technologies, such as the Internet and electronic mail, are embedded in the daily interaction of employees, it is important to have
   guidelines for usage so that these services are
   used properly and not abused.

5. A discussion of how technology helps to integrate the key elements of most businesses: people, processes, and technology.

BUSINESS ROLES AND RESPONSIBILITIES

As a businessperson, you certainly would not want technology people creating technology for the mere sake of it, would you? Well, to the opposite extreme, the nontechnology organizations in many companies often take a hands-off position when it relates to managing technology issues or projects. This is one of the contributing causes to why projects fail expectations. The bottom line is that the managers need to be as concerned about technology implementations being successful as the people developing the systems or integrating those purchased. So, what *exactly* is required? The major responsibilities of the management are detailed hereafter.

Understanding the Role of Technology in the Company

As mentioned at the outset of the book, technology exists in every facet of a company's operations and has an increasingly important role in our day-to-day lives. Therefore, although it may sound trite, it is important that managers take an active role in establishing the strategy and managing the overall use of technology. This role cannot be a casual one in which the manager relies exclusively on the technology organization for decisions and direction. Instead, it has to be planned and discovered together.

Participate in Defining the Requirements for Systems

Managers need to participate with the technology group in defining requirements for the system. Those of us who have worked on these joint efforts know that the first few attempts at nailing down the requirements are usually quite painful. The technology people focus on the technical issues, causing the businesspeople to wonder if their needs will ever be met. Nonetheless, the businesspeople must stay the course. They need to be engaged from the start, insist on prototypes, and, ultimately, sign off on the requirements.

Make sure that the people who are assigned to work with the technology people are realistic about the project. Too often, many of the system requirements are wish-list items that require a significant amount of effort to write the software for and are not necessary for the performance of the business process. This requires that the people who are assigned to the project be able to step outside of how things are done in the current operation and, instead, focus on what is really needed.

Take Joint Ownership for Successes and Failures

Murphy's Law intervenes in many technology projects. At a minimum, there will be some sort of problems that will cause tension between the systems development staff and the business users. What often happens is that the requirements were completed late, unexpected features needed to be developed, or the estimates were overoptimistic. What then typically follows is quite ugly. The technology people start to blame the business for nebulous requirements and blame each other for mismanagement, poor project management, and a misguided selection of software and hardware. The businesspeople often shirk all responsibility and blame the technology people for screwing the whole thing up.

Finger-pointing can be avoided if there is joint ownership for the results of any IT endeavor. If everyone involved is equally on the hook, there is a much better chance that a common solution will be found: schedules will be adjusted, budgets amended, and requirements rephrased. This will keep the teams motivated and secure, leading to a successful implementation.

Becoming as Educated as Possible on Technology

One of the key problems confronting most businesses is the overall lack of knowledge that most of the staff has regarding technology. Most of the people in the workplace grew up in a time in which computers were a rarity. Even people who graduated from college ten years ago barely had exposure to the PC. In fact, if they had any exposure, it was usually a negative experience.

It is important that workers be retooled to work with computer systems. It is critical to break through the resistance that usually comes out of fear or discomfort. Instead, people need to be trained and helped to feel comfortable with computers and how they benefit the workplace.

 Use the people new to your organization as catalysts. Recent college graduates grew up with word processors, spreadsheets, and in many cases, database systems. They will be educated users of technology who could help ease the relationship with the technology staff because they know the lingo better. Just imagine, the next wave will be Internet savvy as well.

 ## ESTABLISHING CRITICAL ROLES IN THE IT GROUP TO MAKE PROJECTS WORK

Even though the responsibility for failed projects is assumed by both the businesspeople and the IT group, for the IT department to succeed, they need to adopt several roles and responsibilities.

Hire People Who Are Both Good Businesspeople and Technologists

It is critical for the businesspeople to ensure that the technology department has people that have a broad view of both technology and business skills. These people need to relate to both sides, so they are often very difficult to find. It is in this area that the new tech-MBA programs will become most important. Many of the students have undergraduate degrees in computer science and electrical engineering, and they pursue MBAs to round out their skills.

 One of the real tricks is to have people who can interface equally as well with the businesspeople and the technology people. Often, as computer people learn the business, their technical skills wane.

 Involve businesspeople in the interviewing and selection process for candidates. In many technology roles in which the person is going to interact frequently with the businesspeople, it is as important, or more so, that the businesspeople accept and endorse the new employee as it is for the technology folks to do. This helps quite a bit if things end up not working out.

Stellar Performer: Denis O'Leary

Denis O'Leary, executive vice president and CIO of Chase Manhattan, is an accomplished technology leader. At Chase, he has worked diligently at building a strong partnership between the business and IT. He worked with other senior managers to form a business technology management council. As Leary explains it, "Every major project has joint ownership." This type of executive-level partnership that is pushed down to other levels helps to ensure that technology decisions are shared among the IS and the business units.

Establish Formal Roles within the Department to Work with the Business

The information system department cannot treat the role of business liaison as an informal, ad hoc position. Instead, the organization should focus on creating a formal position. These relationships need to happen at all levels, from the very strategic to the day-to-day systems requirements.

Several companies have employed people in these positions to serve as those similar to account representatives. For example, in many financial services firms, there are technology people assigned to cover the business units in a similar fashion to the way the investment bankers cover external clients. These people own everything about the relationship, including strategy, tactics, and financial components.

 Often, people at the more senior positions, who have had experience in the business, are excellent candidates for the position of liaison. They are already in good standing with the company's management group, and they understand the business and will help get things started off on the right foot quickly and efficiently.

Ensure That Requirements Are Clear and Formalized

The absolute worst thing that plagues most projects is a mismatch of requirements—what you thought you were getting is not what you get. In life, we are all used to this type of disappointment, and we should expect it with systems as well. Fortunately, it is fairly easy to minimize the downsides to this. Simply put, it is critical to catch these problems as close to the beginning of the project as possible.

The technology group should clearly articulate the components and features of the system and have the business units sign off on them. There are always some gray areas, but there are ways around those.

Ensure That Systems Are Delivered Using an Iterative Development Approach

In my last book, *Successful Reengineering,* I stressed the importance and practicalities of developing computer systems in an iterative fashion.[1] This is truer than ever. Systems efforts that go for the big-bang approach have a greater chance of failure for several reasons. The spirit of this approach is to build and deliver systems (the more complicated, the more relevant this is) a piece at a time and to deliver real functionality to the end users along the way. There are various mechanisms to use, such as introduction to a few users, building pieces of the application that work alongside existing systems, or having users work hand-in-hand with the development staff during the development phase.

Let Those That Want to Remain Technical Stay Technical

Technology managers need to create room and opportunities for those people who want to work in technical areas throughout their career. Not all technologists make for good managers and leaders. In fact, some of the greatest people failures occur, because the best technicians are moved from doing technical work to management. They are usually forced in this direction, because the only way to advance in the organization is via some type of management track. Force your company to adopt a technical track in the organization, in which the senior computer technologists can grow their technical skills and not be penalized for doing so.

Prototyping does not mean hack together. Be careful that the computer people are putting together prototypes based on underlying technologies that can be used to make the system ready for production. Often what you see is not what you can get. Snazzy mock-ups of user interfaces do not necessarily scale to complete applications that work reliably. These types of mock-ups should be used to facilitate the end-user functions wherever possible, not to validate robustness of the architecture or data quality.

RECOGNIZING WHEN A CRITICAL PROJECT MAY MISS ITS DEADLINES

We have all experienced it. The fatal news that a key information system deliverable will not be met. This may delay a product introduction, a key factory improvement, important links to a supplier. The bad news is where it all starts, quickly followed by an exhaustive round of finger-pointing. Blame, of course, makes some people feel better, but it does not get the system delivered. There are some common causes why system deliverables are not met. We will outline them below. There are also some early warning signs that an astute manager can get some insight from.

Poor Estimation Up Front

Information technology managers are not always the best project managers. Too often, human resources are planned for 100 percent usage, in spite of the fact that there are departmental activities, nonproject interrupts, vacations, resignations, new hires, and a whole bunch more things that come up during the course of a project. Planning for resources not to be available more than 60 to 70 percent is a more realistic viewpoint.

In addition, many times, computer people trying to push a technology agenda are overly ambitious in terms of what can be achieved and when. This optimism is a trait found in many programmers and project managers in the technology field.

Changing or Shifting Requirements

Ah, "scope creep," the evil of all computer system projects. The system that starts off with 50 features throughout the project explodes to 100 or even more. This occurs due to a myriad of factors such as:

- **Inadequate planning up front**—Sometimes, there is no formal requirements process, and the systems people just start the project. In this case, the requirements come in over time. The original end dates in this scenario are virtually worthless.

- **Lack of discipline in managing ongoing requirements**—Where there is a tidy formal requirements process, there is often no discipline and no managing the flow of new requirements once the start gun has sounded. If there is no group of people responsible for moderating the "feature set," it is usually not long before Betty from finance and John from accounts payable start lobbying in their additional pet features. This causes bloat and an ever changing target to shoot for. A group or steering committee is required for all projects, to moderate and to ensure that only needed features are delivered.

- **Too large of an initial implementation**—We touch on this topic throughout different parts of this book. Essentially, the maxim is that the larger the project in terms of length, number of lines of computer code, number of features, the more difficult it will be to plan for accurate end dates. Projects that fit in any of these categories have a tremendous risk not to come in on schedule.

- **Vendor dependence**—Computer projects that are dependent on outside providers of software, hardware, and, in some cases, expertise are prone to have delays. This especially occurs when vendor deliverables are on the critical path for the system deliverable. We all laud Microsoft for being the world's most successful software company, but I cannot remember a time when they were on target for meeting a critical release date. So, expecting external vendors to come through is a fairly dangerous path to go down.

- **Staff morale**—For the business manager, this may be the easiest and best way to figure out if a project is in jeopardy. Just go speak to some of the systems people working on the project. If their mood is upbeat, then things are probably going fairly well. If they complain about management, long hours, or appear generally despondent, there is most often a bleak future for the project.

DANGER! Although the morale of the systems people is an accurate weather bell for things to come, you must be careful. Computer professionals (this is a broad stereotype) are among the most pessimistic group of people on the planet. As mentioned before, they are optimistic at the start of projects, and then they grow to become pessimistic about the project and other things as projects go on. Knowing this is important. It is critical that you speak to more than a couple of project members and be careful not to overreact until you are positive that the information received is accurate.

- **Shifting end dates (the old shifting-the-schedule-around trick)**—The savvy project manager will be prudent about capturing changing requirements and vendor delays in an ever changing schedule. This tactic, which is undoubtedly not malicious, appears to be extremely professional, but it can cause a great amount of havoc when looked at in its entirety.

  You are sitting in the biweekly project review meeting, and the project manager passes out the latest copy of the Gantt chart. He starts off by saying everything is going well, except that we just found out that Vendor X is going to be two weeks late with the next production version of their product. This, of course, will delay the final end date by two weeks. You sit back and think. Well, we can afford a few weeks' delay. After all, these people are rather forthcoming. No big deal. A few months go by and another surprise slips in. Then, a few weeks later, before you know it, the project is several months off track, and the whole thing seemed uneventful.

  Delays are just part of any business, and jumping up and down after the first legitimate setback is probably not wise. However, just because there is a competent project manager and a well-articulated schedule, do not be fooled into believing things will be okay. It is the job of the businesspeople to manage the expectations and to provide guidance when these bumps in the road are hit.

- **Loss of key people**—Carefully monitor the resignations and transfers of the computer people working on your project. Of course, at the outset of the project, ensure that you know who the key people are to ensuring the project is successful. Clearly, the loss of even one key person can jeopardize the best-planned projects. Not only should this information be monitored, but, in addition, periodic meetings with these key project people will go miles to ensure that the people have a vested interest in success, that they know you care, and to make sure that the project is successful.

- **Experience with technologies**—Although businesspeople are not expected to be technologists, awareness about what the IT uses from a technology point of view is imperative to understanding project risk. Clearly, when venturing into new platforms or unfamiliar technologies, there is a greater risk that the project may have problems. Ask these questions early on, and ensure that your project does not suffer unknowingly from a lack of experience. This experience has three dimensions. First, is the staff experienced with the technology at your company or elsewhere? Second, is the management experienced with the technology at your company or elsewhere? Third, is your company experienced with the technology? Often, there are nuances in company cultures that cannot be overcome just by hiring experienced veterans or consultants.

COMPUTER PEOPLE ARE DIFFERENT—THEY NEED TO BE TREATED DIFFERENTLY

Without providing reams of psychological or even scientific data, I can say with confidence that most people who build computer systems are different than the average Joe working in your company. Most businesspeople already know this, given the weird, sometimes surreal, experience they have when trying to figure out what to do in the new system or in dealing with an operational problem with a PC.

So, what is one to do? It is important to let the computer people be different and treat them well. It takes people with offbeat interests in the interworkings of operating systems and networks to make sure that your company is able to compete in the twenty-first century. These people (especially the best of them) need to be nurtured like any budding artist, given room to explore, succeed, and fail. Just make sure that there are effective liasions between the technology and business departments.

MOVING BEYOND THE BUZZWORDS OF QUALITY AND REENGINEERING TO THE REAL USE OF TECHNOLOGY TO EFFECT BUSINESS CHANGE

Living through the 1990s with the gurus and consultants beating their chests to the mantra of total quality management and reengineering has made many managers cynical of the use of technology to radically change the business. The mere thought of the phrase *enabling technology* makes one's stomach a bit uneasy.

Nevertheless, technology has been critical to the radical transformation of many business processes. Industries such as telecommunications totally revamped their processes and the computer systems to support those processes to radically improve operations centers and provisioning intervals. The volume of trades that the stock exchanges can handle would be impossible in a day, not so long ago, when the technology was not nearly as mature. These are a few of the countless examples of how technology has transformed businesses.

Make sure that fundamental goals of the business are understood and that the business processes as outlined will help achieve those goals. After this is done, technology can be applied to support the business and the processes. It can never be a substitute for them.

COMPANIES MUST HAVE CLEAR POLICIES ON USAGE OF ELECTRONIC MAIL

Electronic mail has become, perhaps, the most prevalent form of communication within and between companies throughout the world. The words "give me a call" have been replaced with "send me an E-mail." The benefits of this full-time, electronic connectedness comes with quite a few risks for the corporate manager.

Employees can use the E-mail for personal use, as well as inappropriate use. In addition, connections to outside the company allow for all types of messages to be forwarded into the company. Some of these messages are clearly inappropriate with racial, religious, or other offensive overtones. Other times, companies are bombarded or "spammed" with the electronic equivalent to junk mail. People hawking travel opportunities or new products can target people at your company with one fell swoop. These types of messages create challenges for all managers throughout the firm.

First, let's deal with inappropriate messages. Throughout the last year, several companies have been sued, because employees have used electronic mail to forward potentially offensive messages that originated outside the firm to employees inside the firm. This is a double-edged sword. Clearly, it would be almost ridiculous to monitor every electronic message that comes into the firm for inappropriate content, similar to the guards examining the mail of prisoners. And, at the same time, companies need these outside connections to communicate with suppliers and customers. Beyond that, it is nearly impossible to stop employees from doing stupid things. In addition, from a legal perspective, the life span of an electronic mail message creates unique problems that companies did not face when the telephone was the only form of communications.

Therefore, it must be clear that the electronic mail systems are for business use only. In that spirit, any personal, inappropriate, or illegal use of the system must be considered an offense that could lead to termination. This type of simple statement helps establish the ground rules for the use of the systems and properly sets the expectations for employees.

Second, spamming is a serious problem for corporate and IT managers alike. In many companies, message traffic is extremely high already, without adding extra, unwanted messages to the mix. This increases stress on the technology infrastructure to deliver needless messages. Since there are typically no easy ways to prioritize message traffic, most companies use first-come-first-serve. Thus, a message critical to the business may be delayed by unwanted messages from the outside. Companies can combat this by ensuring that messages from outside the firm cannot be targeted to large mailgroups and that instrumentation on the source of messages is used to ensure that the same sender is not flooding the corporate network.

DO NOT LET ELECTRONIC MAIL REPLACE FACE-TO-FACE COMMUNICATION

DANGER!

For all the benefits of electronic mail, one of the key problems with the technology is that it is often used as a substitute for required face-to-face communication. There are times when a

Stellar Performer: VeriFone

VeriFone makes money as a company with a leadership position in electronic payments by handling over one-half of an $800 billion U.S. market in electronic transactions. Recently, they made news by being bought by Hewlett-Packard.

Operationally, VeriFone exists as a company with a central nervous system consisting of one of the simplest technologies, electronic mail. Note—this example condones the opposite suggestion made later that E-mail can be an enemy within a company, subject to various abuses, just trying to be balanced. The 2,500-plus employees of VeriFone and the processes that are used are an extension of the electronic mail system.

At VeriFone, there are no paper or secretaries to be found. Each employee is linked together via E-mail worldwide 24 hours a day. There is seamless communication at all levels of the corporation. Decisions are made via E-mail, and employees are encouraged to send messages to anyone who can help, regardless of level in the organization. In addition, employees can choose to send E-mail to everyone if the occasion warrants it. VeriFone does not have the same problems that other companies have with abuse of the E-mail system, mostly because it has become a social system for how the company behaves and operates. Each person takes the form and the messages sent seriously.

Another important facet of VeriFone's business is that they are insensitive to time and distance, as explained by CEO Hatim Tyabji.

If you are operating by conventional means—phone or fax or whatever—you have to know where someone is to work with them. The way we operate, it doesn't make any difference where people are. I don't give a damn where they are, as long as they can access E-mail. We have also proven that there is no reason VeriFone can't have a 24-hour day. VeriFone does have a 24-hour day—and without people pulling all-nighters or getting so frazzled they can't function. We have software projects that basically follow the sun. Our facility in Bangalore, India, is one of our centers of excellence for networking and communications. So Bangalore develops the communications code for new products. Of course, that code has to be tested, and that work is done in Dallas. It also has to be integrated into our overall systems code, and that work is often done in Hawaii, where many of our systems engineers are based. In a conventional company, where all the engineers are sitting in the same place, you'd have a tremendous amount of serial processing. First, you write the code, then you test it, then you integrate it. Here, because our people are

(Continued)

(Continued)

distributed around the world, everything works in parallel. Before they go to sleep, the boys in Bangalore upload code and ship it to, say, Dallas or Hawaii, let those guys work on it, and then they start again the next morning in Bangalore. Allowing our projects to follow the sun is something that we have done consistently—and with devastating efficiency.

Of course, without technology linking the various parts of the company together, these streamlined 24-hour processes would not be possible. Through robust computer networks, all corporate information is available on-line, worldwide, for immediate access. The company's top 250 people, for example, track down sales to the last week, the last day, even the last hour. Another database tracks which people speak what languages—a useful tool for solving the day-to-day communication headaches that come from doing business around the world. Another system posts the travel itineraries of everyone in the company, including flight details, hotel reservations, and phone numbers.

Source: Fast Company, 1, no. 1 (November 1995): 115.

person will send a mail message to another person who is an office or a cube away rather than getting up to visit that person. While this is sometimes an effective, electronic equivalent to a Post-it note, often it is a sign of other dysfunctional behavior at the company. To this point, there are two classifications of problems that are coming from overuse or misuse of electronic mail.

People avoiding one another—Throughout many companies, you will find employees that use E-mail as a mechanism to avoid working with peers that they may not agree with, people in other departments that they loathe, and, in some cases, customers with whom contact is critical. This is a big problem. It is important that people spend time face-to-face to solve issues quickly, build relationships, and to eliminate possible tensions. A culture in which E-mail is used as a replacement for this direct contact leads to isolated employees who do not build the necessary teams required to deliver product in a speedy and quality way.

Interview with Hatim Tyabji of VeriFone, Inc.

Eric Nee

UPSIDE: Is electronic commerce still in its infancy? TYABJI: Electronic commerce today is in its embryonic stages. Generally, the growth of a new business is more evolutionary than revolutionary, and new trends and new approaches always seem to take a heck of a lot longer than what people prognosticate.

But if you look at the growth of the Internet and the World Wide Web over the last 18 or 24 months, nobody would have projected that it would have grown as fast as it has and gained so much cachet.

It took 10 or 15 years for VeriFone and others to establish electronic credit card authorization and transactions. Five to seven years. But there, the growth of the infrastructure was in the physical space. That infrastructure had to be established, and since it was a physical infrastructure, equipment had to be shipped, merchants had to be equipped and so on. The big difference is that the establishment of a virtual infrastructure is much faster and far easier than the establishment of a physical infrastructure.

The other element is that the key players in the electronic payments industry—the card associations, financial institutions and merchants—have gotten used to the utilization of electronics, so embracing electronic payments in the virtual space is going to come faster than in the physical space.

The third key element is that there is almost a complete one-to-one mapping in the physical infrastructure and the channels of distribution. You can have the most wonderful ideas in the world and the most wonderful technologies in the world, but if you don't have the appropriate channels of distribution and if those channels of distribution will not embrace your technology, you're going to get nowhere very fast.

The same card associations that established the rules and the interchange rates that facilitated the physical space are doing exactly the same thing in the virtual space.

(Continued)

(Continued)

What needs to happen for electronic commerce to be accepted widely? Some of the impediments are intangible and some are tangible. One of the intangible elements that has to be overcome by the industry is to get consumers to have confidence in the conduction of electronic payments in the virtual space.

Today you don't think anything of taking one of your credit cards or debit cards and going to an ATM machine somewhere in France or the United Kingdom, putting your American card into the machine, and withdrawing 500 francs or 600 deutsche marks. But all of that structure has happened because merchants and consumers have a belief in the security. They have a belief that somebody's not going to fleece them. That state of mind needs to be achieved in the virtual space. Our approach is not to take some foolish method whereby we say we've got the best technology. We work with Visa and Master-Card to facilitate the formation of standards. Visa and MasterCard have now come forward with SET [secure electronic transaction]. We announced in June that we are the first systems house in the world that is going to implement it.

As we implement SET, some of our competition will stand up and say SET is not complete. My response is very straightforward. No standard can be complete at the theoretical level. A standard is only complete when somebody has the guts to go forward and start to implement it.

Are there any technical impediments to electronic commerce? I'd be foolish if I said there weren't technical impediments. But are they rocket science? Is it 1960 and are we talking about putting a man on the moon by the end of the decade? Good God, no. From a technical standpoint, I worry. But then, I worry about everything.

How long will it take for the consumer and merchant to have confidence in the Internet payment system? The same institutions that made the physical space happen—the card associations and the financial institutions—have embraced this. As they launch educational campaigns, their word will cause the consumer and merchant to embrace it, I would say within the next two to five years.

The one thing people are struggling over now is, how do you map cash from the physical world to the virtual

(Continued)

(Continued)

world? You seem to believe that solving the credit and debit card issue is the first problem to tackle. Ninety-nine percent or 99.9 percent of cash payments are not automated in the physical world. The automation of cash payments is something people started talking about well before the virtual space existed. [They started looking at it because] the stream of income that financial institutions have in the physical space occurs because they are automating transactions, and they're able to charge x pennies for their transactions.

If you look at the U.S., about 16 percent of payments occur in the credit, debit and check area, and 84 percent of all payments occur in the cash area. Financial institutions started to realize that everybody was fighting over the 16-percent space, and the 84-percent space was left completely fallow.

Are those percentages measuring numbers of transactions or dollar value? Number of transactions. At the end of the day, it's the number of transactions that causes the income flow for the financial institution. So there has been a fair amount of interest, not too surprisingly, as to how the 84 percent of the market in the physical space is going to be automated.

The smart card is starting to come into its own. The reasons for that are fairly straightforward. Up until the mid-'80s, you had chip cards that cost more than $5. On the other hand, magnetic stripe cards cost 30 cents. You had a huge worldwide infrastructure that was geared to magnetic stripe cards, and tens of billions of magnetic stripe cards were issued.

But a couple of things have happened over the last three to five years. Number one is that the cost of chip cards is dropping dramatically. Number two, the technology of chip cards is changing. As semiconductor technology has gone up in complexity and down as far as the cost curve is concerned, you're able to put a huge amount of RAM on the chip and utilize chip cards for loyalty-based transactions.

Loyalty-based transactions? The ability [for merchants] to say, "The more you come back to my shop the more you will be rewarded."

Supermarkets are looking at this and saying, "Well, if you utilize chip cards, is a person more liable to come to a Safeway than he or she might be otherwise?" If the experience of the airlines and hotels and car rental companies is any guide, then the answer is yes.

(Continued)

(Continued)

The third element, driven largely from outside the U.S., is this phenomenon of stored value cards, which in layman's terms is 100 percent cash replacement. When you go to a newspaper kiosk and buy *The New York Times* or *The Wall Street Journal,* rather than fishing in your pocket to find the exact change, you are able to utilize chip cards.

We are cognizant of what is going on around the world, and we're engaged in [smart card] pilots in the Netherlands, the Czech Republic and in certain countries in Asia. But the operative word is "pilots." In spite of all of the press and all the arm-waving, there has not been a nationwide rollout in any country, although we believe that it'll happen. Will it happen first in the physical space? That is our belief. Given the rate of change and the growth in the virtual space, there may be some degree of parallelism.

What role does VeriFone play in smart cards? You don't need to be on-line to a financial institution to do a transaction. Our role continues to be that of a systems house. Whether that solution happens to be off-line or on-line is totally irrelevant. The solutions we provide today are geared to the utilization of magnetic stripe cards because that's what the infrastructure is geared toward. We provide all of the end-to-end system solutions, as well as the hardware and application software that facilitate them. Our approach to chip cards is identical.

There are very few countries with a telecommunications infrastructure as robust and as cheap as it is in our country. In the U.K., the structure's robust, but it's very expensive. And then you've got countries where the telecommunications infrastructure, politely stated, is almost nonexistent. In those kinds of situations, off-line [makes sense] big time.

The Internet products VeriFone announced in June include three elements: vGATE, vPOS and vWALLET. Could you tell me exactly what vWALLET is, because it ties in to some of the issues of electronic cash. vWALLET is a virtual wallet [that resides] on your PC. When you go into vWALLET you'll have credit or debit cards. Then you go to the merchant space. The vPOS, or virtual point-of-sale terminal, is in the merchant's server.

How will you distribute the vPOS to the merchant? The channel of distribution today for the physical device is the financial institutions. They have a sales force that calls on merchants, because that's their bread-and-butter business. They want the merchant tied

(Continued)

(Continued)

to the bank. We'll have exactly the same thing in the virtual space. The field organization will provide merchants with a diskette as opposed to a physical terminal.

Companies like Netscape are also going to those merchants and trying to sell them a virtual merchant solution. Certainly. But that'd be like saying that in the physical space, VeriFone is going to sell the terminal to the merchant. The merchant has to have a financial institution relationship, whether Netscape or VeriFone goes in. You can't bypass the financial institution, unless you're going to become one. All we are doing is leveraging the very strong relationships we have with the financial institutions in the physical space into the virtual space.

How do you get vWALLET to the consumer? Probably by downloading it packaged with the browser. We've signed alliances with both Netscape and Oracle, in the browser area and the server area. It is not our intent to compete with Netscape or Oracle. We're not a server company. I'm not going to come up with a Netscape Navigator. It makes an enormous amount of strategic sense for Veri-Fone to stick to its core competencies in the payment technology area and to leverage its core competencies by aligning, combining our payment technology with their servers.

Will Netscape bundle vWALLET with its browser? That is something that we are working with them on, as we're working with Oracle.

On another topic, how do you make money on the Internet? Do you sell your software to the merchants and the bank in a one-time sale, or do you get some sort of ongoing fee? Our fundamental business model, right from the get-go, has not been to compete with our customers. Our business model is not on a per-transaction basis. That's the business model of our financial institutions. We provide the technology, in this particular case the software, and we expect to make our money in the context of the sale and licensing of the software, just the way that a Microsoft or a Netscape makes money.

You mentioned that one of the interesting things about e-cash is the possibility of anyone creating it. Doesn't it

(Continued)

(Continued)

open up the game as to who is a bank, who is not a bank, who creates the money? The leverage that the Visas and Wells Fargos have in today's credit-debit world might go away. Whenever you go through a sea change in technology it opens up the situation, and then it's the one who is not faint of heart and who's prepared to step in and take advantage of the situation that is going to prevail. I think that depending on what kind of regulations come down and what kind of opportunities there are, it is entirely possible that the financial institutions and the card associations will maintain their dominant position. Or there may be a shifting of the sands.

We work very closely with card associations and financial institutions around the world, and I would say that there is a very rich appreciation in that constituency of what is happening in the Internet space. They realize that if they don't aggressively move forward, they may be left behind, and I do not believe they will be left behind.

How do you run your company? A lot of companies talk today about being virtual in the organizational sense, as opposed to the Internet sense. I'm not aware of any company that has truly taken what it believes in and put it in action. For us, it's a way of life. The mind-set in [VeriFone] is different, and it affords us enormous competitive advantages. When I send an E-mail to our staff it goes to every man, woman and child in the company, wherever he or she happens to be. I am 100 percent sure that 12 hours from the time I press that button everybody has seen it.

Conventional wisdom says every company has a headquarters. The definition of a headquarters is where the chief executive is based, and all of the decisions emanate from there. I think that's a bunch of garbage. I think the real decision making and the real wisdom comes from the people. You won't see any mahogany splendor here [at VeriFone]. We bought our furniture at a sale in Taipei because we couldn't afford to buy furniture in the U.S. It's adequate, it's not exceptional. I'll probably never replace it. It sends a signal, doesn't it? You look around, and you'll see that kind of spartan thinking, which I believe is very crucial. Spartan doesn't have to be ugly, by the way.

My vice president of human resources, Katherine Beall, is based in Dallas. Our executive vice president for development of manufacturing, Jim Palmer, is based in Costa Mesa, California. People are scattered all over. It works. My development centers are scattered all over the world. Why? Because that's where the talent is.

(Continued)

(Continued)

Is there a tension between having a company that's disparate and keeping it focused? It's a fallacy that it's easier to talk to people on a campus, because most people, if they're in Building 1, will go to Building 2 maybe once a year. They never go to Building 2. Now, is it a challenge? Absolutely.

We've been running the company this way since the mid-'80s because the infrastructure has been there. Things that people talk about today, like the intranet, have been articles of faith with us before the terms existed.

But you meet with your executive staff every six weeks? Yes. You can have all the technology in the world, but what makes human beings click is rapport, chemistry. You can't have teamwork unless people are together. Every once in a while someone says, "You've got all this technology and you operate the company in a virtual way, but it's a real paradox that you travel 80 to 90 percent of the time." I don't see any paradox in that whatsoever. You can't provide leadership through memos. Omar Bradley, on that last drive into Germany, was called the "GI General." That's because he was visible. He was on the front lines. He didn't sit back in some cushy headquarters issuing commands. That's why Bradley became a five-star general. I believe that kind of leadership is required, and that's the reason I travel as much as I do. I've got personal contact with all my customers. I've got personal contact with my people, and I believe in being very visible. I expect my staff to do the same thing.

Because of your network, you're able to know on a daily basis how the business is doing by looking at orders and sales and costs. Do you find that to be useful or is that more information than one needs? You [have to] have information, not data. I'm sure some folks in the company find that it's not useful daily, and so they use it weekly or monthly, and there are some who find it useful every half a day.

I've read that a large number of your employees are classified as "insiders." I don't know the exact number [of insiders], but it's several hundred. But that comes down to one word: trust. In most companies you'll have five or six people who are insiders.

Is it difficult for people who come from other companies to adjust to VeriFone, particularly if they've been in a man-

(Continued)

(Continued)

**agement role, used to having more control over informa-
tion and people?** It varies from person to person. In some cases it's
like a bucket of cold water in your face, because we work very differently. We live very differently. Those who don't relate to it [at the
beginning] never relate to it. We are very intense and extremely
passionate. There's no in-between.

It's somewhat self-selecting in that way. It is self-selecting. I
have been asked in the past, "Given the kind of culture you have,
what are your recruitment methods?" We haven't found any holy
grails.

**Do you still like to have employees clustered in work
groups, or can they increasingly work out of their homes?**
There are some shades of gray. In certain projects, and depending on
what kind of technology or time frame we're talking about, I think
there is no question that you can substitute the team, or the cluster-
ing as you call it. When you've got a team of 15 engineers and they
want to get this thing out by the 15th of July, there's a tremendous
self-reinforcing mechanism of sharing the pizza late at night and
sharing the Coke in the morning. If you have the same 15 people
scattered in their homes, they're not sharing the pizzas at night and
they're not having the dialogue, and it just is not the same. You can't
discount or not take into account the human element of the situation.

Source: Eric Nee, Interview with Hatim Tyabji of Verifone, Inc., Upside *magazine (September
1996).*

*Editor's Note: In June 1997, VeriFone agreed to a $1.3 billion merger with
Hewlett-Packard Co. VeriFone is now a wholly owned subsidiary of HP. Tyabji
remains president and CEO of the subsidiary. Eric Nee, formerly editor of* Upside
magazine, is now Silicon Valley bureau chief for Forbes *magazine.*

Mixed messages due to the lack of sensitivity of E-mail—People cannot see the expression on your face or hear the tone of your voice when you send them an E-mail message. Res ipsa loquitor. In this case, the words speak for themselves. Much like great literature or a poem, there is a wide range of interpretation that can take place when reading messages. Was the person being sincere, sarcastic, cutting, or merely attempting to be friendly or cute? It is up to the reader to determine. Thus, we have all seen what happens. Employees speculate as to the meaning of messages, often get angry, and sometimes engage in E-mail war, frequently referred to as flaming. This is clearly unproductive.

 Charles Wang, CEO of Computer Associates, actually has the firm's electronic mail system completely shut down for several hours a day. His thinking? This is an opportunity for people to do other work and to get out and see people in the organization. Wang believes this practice increases productivity.

 USE OF THE INTERNET IS A PRIVILEGE, NOT A RIGHT

Growing up, many of us were taught that driving a motor vehicle is a privilege, not a right. If we broke the law, our ability to drive would be taken away, and our lives would become quite miserable. The same approach needs to be taken for using the Internet.

Many companies, to improve employee productivity, to work with suppliers and customers, and, in some cases, just because it is the cool thing to do, have jumped on the bandwagon of providing Internet connections for use by employees. Recent studies show that 50 percent of U.S. companies have external Web sites.[2]

This push of this new technology has created a difficult situation for managers. The ability for employees to overuse the Internet for personal reasons when they are supposed to be working exists, as does the possibility of people using the Internet for inappropriate reasons altogether. This creates a challenge for managers. The desire is to ensure that people are happy and productive. Spying on them usually makes them neither. However, allowing the whole situation to go unchecked borders on being irresponsible.

One approach that a company can take is to establish policies for Internet use. Companies should explicitly state in code-of-conduct documentation what its policy for use of the Internet is. Thus, it should be clear to employees that the Internet, like any other corporate technology, is to be used for company business only and not for personal or inappropriate behavior. In practice, like many things, the possible negative ramifications are slight for personal use and grave for inappropriate uses.

So, the challenge is in how these policies are enforced. The widespread use of the Internet has created opportunities for many software companies to develop programs that trap usage of the Internet, as well as what sites are being visited. This software is much like the ability that most telephone equipment has to capture detailed call records, similar to what shows up on a person's phone bill. In the corporate world, this software can be used for spying on employees to catch violators of the policy, help plan for capacity, or even as a charge back mechanism for Internet usage.

In monitoring Internet usage, it is probably best to use collection software on an auditing basis. Much like the Internal Revenue Service, from time to time, randomly pick a set of employees and check the data. This is much less expensive than employing people to act as security agents, monitoring all the time, looking for bad guys.

To stop the use of the Internet for inappropriate reasons, work with a company that monitors sexual offense and illegal sites, and install software to block their access. This is similar to the capability that people have on telephones to block the use of 900-numbers. The investment in a service like this is well worth the money.

USING R&D TO KEEP TECHNOLOGY PEOPLE HAPPY AND FRESH

It should be clear, at this point, that almost every company needs to have competent and motivated computer professionals. As this book illustrates,

Stellar Performer:
The Telecommunications Industry

The telecommunications industry is extremely competitive. Long-distance carriers and local-access providers are battling for customer market share and mind share, while, at the same time, trying to provide new services. The one thing that all of the titans, such as AT&T, US West, MCI, and what seems like a zillion other smaller companies, have in common is that they are all centering in on customer loyalty. Customer turnover, known as churn, is wreaking havoc with telecom profit margins.

The telecom industry is turning to technology to provide relief. In telecommunications, IT doesn't merely support the product. It is the product. Dave Laube, vice president and CIO of US West Communications Co. (which provides local phone service in 14 states), said, "The company doesn't have a product unless IT can bring it to the representatives' screens to sell at the front end and bring it to the billing systems at the back end." Thus, the end-to-end business process of product, support, and billing is enabled in today's telecommunication companies by technology.

One compelling example of a product born of technology, MCI's groundbreaking Friends and Family discount calling program, was built from a jumble of different MCI computer systems integrated to provide intelligent call routing and billing. MCI's systems integration skills have led to a number of different products since then, including MCI One, which consolidates multiple services on one bill for the customer.

These days, systems developers at telecommunication companies are focused on gathering as many services as possible—such as local phone service, cellular service, and Internet access—together on a single bill. So-called bundling operates on a basic assumption: Customers who sign up for more than one service with a single carrier are less likely to switch. Today, with multiple discount plans and bundled services coming to the fore, telecommunication companies have a powerful need to integrate information from myriad applications and systems, none of which knows how to talk to the others.

At the back end of these technology changes are service centers that allow for representatives to view customer information in a consolidated way, as well as operations centers that use sophisticated technology to ensure that the networks that allow for intelligent routing in the like are highly available. On the front end, sales and marketing comb through large data warehouses to find reasons why customers stay or customers leave so that ad campaigns and service can be changed to support the need to retain customers.

Source: CIO *magazine (1 June 1997).*

even the most basic business operations require computer people to ensure they perform with the appropriate level of quality and consistency. Unfortunately, computer professionals, unlike the processes that they facilitate, will not perform consistently over time doing the same types of tasks. In fact, many top-notch computer people get bored doing the same types of things with the same types of technology—and some very quickly.

Spending money on R&D is an easy way to keep computer people interested in staying with your company and not wanting to move on at the first sign of boredom. Insist that a percentage of the technology budget be dedicated to work with more advanced technologies that may or may not have a direct or, at least, short-term business impact. How should this be done?

- Identify key technologists—This should be easy. We know our star performers and technology aficionados.

- Understand technology market trends and potential fit to your business—This involves a bit more work here. If there is a technology strategy group in your organization, they should have the answer. If not, consultants and research groups, such as Gartner, can provide some help.

- Develop R&D initiatives—Choose several projects that combine the latest or leading-edge technologies with areas that your firm could potentially gain strategic advantage. Currently, the area that is most obvious relates to Internet technologies. However, there could be areas, such as data warehousing and supply chain technologies, that would be equally appropriate. It is important to take a venture capitalist approach to these efforts—choose several, and maybe one or two will work out for the best.

- Select appropriate people—Pick among strong technologists for each project, trying to ensure that you have a group of people that can work well together

- Start projects—Have some type of plan that gets the projects going, so that it is understood what is entailed.

- Carefully monitor—Management exposure into these projects is important. This is a good opportunity to see how some of the best people solve problems collectively and creatively. In addition, it is through these projects that a possible breakthrough for the business may be achieved. A hands-on approach from management may create a situation in which opportunities that were not obvious at the start can be seized.

- Rotate people next time—Different people should be given a chance to work on these efforts. Do not go to the same source each time unless, of course, you are trying to build a permanent R&D group.

Stellar Performer: Allied Signal

Allied Signal used a rather interesting approach to achieve the goal of keeping technology people fresh, and, at the same time, adding unique business value. They formed a computing technology center where many of the best IT managers and technicians formed an internal SWAT team, tasked with taking on serious challenges facing the company. The idea was to get a focus on issues with some top technology talent. This concept spread into a mainstream organizational paradigm for handling important initiatives. Allied Signal's approach for setting up a computer technology center:

- Select the most qualified people.
- Mix skill base between seasoned professionals and young high potentials with experience in new technology.
- Integrate technologies (take a cross-platform perspective).
- Include technology assessment in the mission.
- Provide appropriate tools and infrastructure.
- Superior leadership.

At Allied Signal, the computer technology center started as a mainframe data center. Before they were done, this group of technologists was given such challenges as implementing E-mail, electronic commerce, and standardizing desktop computers.

Source: The Digital Organization.

4

The Role of Information Technology in the Organization[1]

The world has changed dramatically for the central information technology (IT) organization. This one-time corporate house of power is finding it difficult to adjust to the demands imposed by the new marketplace. This chapter explores why IT is having such a hard time, what the future may hold, and what the corporate manager needs to do to help create a new environment in which the IT department is an active partner in helping the organization realize its goals.

Not too long ago, as late as the early 1990s, the IT organization was an internal cash cow that was holding its customers, the rest of the company, hostage. Systems were delivered when IT staff got around to it. Budgets were consistently overrun. The users just had to deal with it. After all, what choice was there?

Every manager knows the world has changed. The once mighty information systems departments are being pushed around by the business units. If the CIO is lucky, he or she may stick around for more than a couple of years. Although outsourcing has now become a standard part of the IT portfolio, many firms continue to outsource to a third party that is thought to have the wisdom to do things faster, cheaper, and better. Software development is being treated like cafeteria service. This is, indeed, a brave new world.

All this change begs the question, what *is* the future of the IT department? Actually, the question needs to be rephrased to, what *should be* the future for the information systems department? Corporate management, senior information systems management, and information systems professionals will all have critical roles in shaping the future of this function. An examination of the forces tearing at IT organizations reveals that several possible futures are likely. But first, how important is the role of technology anyway?

As the entire premise of this book suggests, IT is intertwined with almost all corporate initiatives. In the early 1990s, corporations and public-sector organizations used IT to reengineer their operations and launch new strategic objectives. Mortgage companies used advanced database and communications capabilities, quickly retrieving and compiling information about applicants. Securities firms continue to create entirely new financial instruments. Many police departments use wireless data technology as a crime-fighting tool, accessing state and national crime databases without using their radios. Sales force automation systems are linked to mobile salespeople with the home office to provide updated product information and faster, more reliable order entry. These corporate initiatives and countless others have only become possible because of sophisticated IT.

Given the rising importance of IT and its focus on improving businesses, it is surprising how far the star for the internal IT shop has fallen, the questioning of the role of IT, and the skepticism that surrounds technology efforts in many companies. One would think that all companies would view IT and the central IT shops that provide it as vital to the existence of the corporation. But the stresses facing IT today are both different and more acute than they have ever been.

WHAT DOES THE IT WORLD LOOK LIKE TODAY?

The world for the internal IT organization is not the same as it once was. The primary reason for this is the change in the climate in which these organizations operate. Three external forces—business transformation, competition, and technology innovations—are requiring the IT organization to evolve.

In the early to mid-1990s, business transformation consisted of many movements, such as reengineering, downsizing, and agility. The common thread was that the marketplace pushed companies to examine the business that they are in and how they are executing core processes. Reengineering demanded more of the IT organization, because it required new skills, techniques, and resources. In 1994, a Computer Sciences Corporation (CSC) Index survey of 600 companies reported that 54 percent of the respondents felt that getting the information systems and technology infrastructure in place was very or extremely difficult. Indeed, reengineering put a strain on the IT organization in three ways. First, it required that the personnel in the IT organization acquire an in-depth knowledge of the business and technology enablers so that they can craft and implement a new vision of operations. Second, new methods, such as rapid prototyping and simulation, were used to demonstrate and validate assumptions to the business units. Third, reengineering projects demanded the analytical and problem-solving skills most often found in the IT organization. These challenges took IT out of its usual comfort zone and forced business-oriented technology innovation.

In recent times, the new realities of the marketplace have added to the strain brought on by change management movements. The volatile nature of business today requires firms to speed up product cycle times, which, in turn, creates a need for faster software development cycles. Also, as firms globalize, systems and data networks require higher availability and increased performance. These new business realities are forcing IT to become better informed on corporate strategies, extremely focused on reducing cycle times, and on top of emerging technologies.

The competitive pressures on the internal IT organization are just as daunting as the business pressures. In his early-1990s book, *Decline and Fall of the American Programmer,* author Ed Yourdon made the claim that off-shore software development can be done faster, with better quality, and for less cost. At the time, this was not surprising, since 50 percent of the computer science

Ph.D. students in the United States are foreign nationals. In fact, the India-based software programming group that Motorola used earned the highest possible rating on a respected technical quality measure developed by the Software Engineering Institute (SEI). In contrast, in measuring over 250 U.S. software houses, 74 percent measured according to the SEI standards achieved the lowest possible rating. Also, it is quite obvious that off-shore software houses are less costly. On Wall Street and in many R&D organizations, a fully loaded technical headcount costs over $200,000 per year. The same headcount in India costs $50,000 to $60,000. Given these cost comparisons alone, it is not surprising that business managers have looked off-shore for traditional IT functions.[2]

At the same time, many companies have looked off-shore to rid themselves of the burden of managing an IT organization altogether. The outsourcing craze has hit full-swing. Traditionally, high-tech Hughes Aircraft and Xerox have handed over their entire IT functions to CSC and Electronic Data Systems, respectively. Even the end users are getting in on the act. Users are building their own powerful PC database, spreadsheet, and workgroup applications with products such as Microsoft Access, Microsoft Excel, and Lotus Notes. They are even designing their own jazzy screens with packages, like Visual Basic. With these options, a firm's IT shop no longer has a stranglehold on all technology initiatives.

Technology changes are also putting a strain on the IT organization. In essence, technology itself is confusing IT, because some technologies are rapidly maturing as others are emerging. The maturing process is evident, because more often than before, IT is being faced with buy-versus-build decisions. Although a large percentage of nonproprietary systems (e.g., payroll, human resources, and general ledger) were, even a few years ago, developed internally, the focus is shifting to purchasing commercially available software in these areas. Many people believe that this was always the intent, but the harsh reality is that every company did things just differently enough so that a custom solution would be required. As long as the dollars were plentiful and competition was not as fierce, this mindset could prevail. Now, the business need to develop software that provides a competitive advantage, coupled with the emergence of products that have matured, is forcing companies to reevaluate the traditional position to build instead of buy. PeopleSoft, a provider of human resource and financial service application products, is an excellent example of a company that has taken advantage of the trend of organizations seriously evaluating the buy-versus-build decision. In addition, the latest round of turnkey products is another place where end users can use their technical prowess. Most third-party, total-solution providers, including PeopleSoft, SAP, and Baan, provide the capability to customize report writing and build applications without extensive assistance from a software development staff.

Although the client server has been around for ten years or so, the migration to this architecture continues to have an effect on the IT organization. The change in skill sets required for the distributed computing model remains difficult for many IT organizations to get a handle on. Just as important as the change in technology is the change in mindset for the IT professional away from centralized computing. As if this adjustment has not been enough, the emergence of workflow software, imaging, document management, and desktop videoconferencing (with a plethora of computing applications built around it) is creating a whole new set of technical challenges for the typical IT organization. All these technologies pale in comparison to the pain for the IT department created by the advent of Internet computing. This is really distributed technology that is pushing the envelope for the IT organization's ability to manage information, implement security, and service a mobile workforce.

THE NEW ROLES FOR THE IT ORGANIZATION

Information technology organizations are facing changing customers, changing competitors, and changing tools. The status quo is certainly not acceptable. For IT organizations to survive, they must make fundamental changes in how they look and what they do. Similarly, a transformation must take place among IT professionals.

Three new roles for the IT organization are rapidly emerging. But there is no guarantee that there will be a natural progression from one role to the next. In fact, elements of all three roles may exist in some companies. The role that an IT organization will play will largely depend on the talents of each organization, the culture of the firm, and the market forces within the vertical industry being supported. Although these roles have not been clearly distinguished for individual organizations, elements of each new role are being seen in many IT organizations across the United States. The three roles are described below.

Business Partners

Futurist Faith Popcorn coined the term *cocooning* to suggest that people will spend more quiet time at home and less time going out for entertainment. Information technology has done its own form of cocooning over the years with the paradigm, "give me your requirement, I'll develop the code and throw it back over the wall," which had prevailed in most organizations. Since this model is now clearly unsatisfactory, IT professionals must become intimate with the business strategy and operations of the company in which they work. In essence, they must break out of their cocoon. Much like managers who profess management by walking around, IT professionals must spend time in the business units, so that they can understand the fundamental nature of the core business. For example, in several telecommunications companies, newly hired engineers and computer scientists spend time in operations, learning how that department works. On Wall Street, many IT professionals are taking trader-licensing exams, so that they will become more acquainted with the business that they support.

Before IT can become a business partner, it must prove that it is a worthy one. Information technology leaders must overcome the myth that expenditures on IT have not boosted overall productivity. They must do this by being able to clearly articulate the benefits of technology to the business, thereby dispelling the productivity paradox. Professor James Quinn of Dartmouth University explains that IT benefits are often best articulated by pointing out the opportunity costs that would be lost without the use of technology. Simply put, there are strategies, growth, and business opportunities that could never be realized without using IT. For example, without sophisticated computer systems, the world's stock markets could never keep up with the number of trades. Point-of-sale and credit card verification technology are other examples of technology breakthroughs that have revolutionized the way many businesses run. It is difficult to imagine how fast-food, supermarkets, and credit card companies would compete without using these technologies. Since they probably could not do so, IT has created a lowest-common-denominator market participation threshold. However, to gain a competitive advantage through the use of IT, companies must far exceed this minimum threshold.

Without being so brash as to say, "you can't live without us," in recent years, some IT organizations created disciplined approaches to justify why they are worthy partners. At Conoco, the oil concern, the IT organization worked with the business units to create value measurements. The value of a system solution is measured by how the technology positively affects different levels of the company: individual, department, and business unit.

Other IT organizations are measuring their value to the new business partnership by borrowing an often-used reengineering concept. These companies are measuring the value of technology based on its impact on business processes. For example, Watkins-Johnson, an electronics firm, demonstrated the value of IT by using an approach that ties value of technology to its impact on business processes in a cost/benefit approach. It looked at the cost of a given system function compared with the benefits to the process expected to be derived from implementing the system change.

Ultimately, for a partnership to develop, the remainder of a business must have a new outlook on IT. Although now a bit outdated in terms of time, the still-relevant 1994 article in the *Sloan Management Review* asked the question, "Is your CIO adding value?" The answers suggested that a CIO can only add value when senior corporate management views the use of IT as strategic to the goals of the business. Although some senior corporate managers are particularly enlightened in this area, others are only influenced when the CIO demonstrates an obsessive and continuous focus on business imperatives.

Change Agents

In the early and mid-1990s, companies spent an unbelievable amount of money on the business of change, in the form of reengineering, restructuring, business transformation, and the like. About all that most management scholars and gurus agree on is that the only certainty in the future is that change will be constant. The pace of change has continued with diversification, a wild stock market, and globalization. Will companies continue to rely on external consultants to help manage change? If change is never ending, is there something preventing IT staff from becoming the new business consultants? Today, the largest amount of change that is taking place is due to technology.

The Internet, global competition, and mobile workforce require technological innovation to enable companies to do things that they could not do without the use of technology. Information technology has the internal intellectual horsepower required to fuel these initiatives. As IT personnel begin to bridge the skills gap in business acumen, they will become better qualified to execute business-focused projects better than inexperienced, nontechnology-savvy, business school graduates. It is easier to teach IT and other technical personnel about the business than it is to teach strictly business-oriented personnel about technology.

The addition of vertical industry business skills will not be enough for IT professionals to become the change agents of the future. Instead, they will need a wide variety of skills—process analysis, computer modeling and simulation, systems integration—to complement their understanding of IT. Much of this orientation is already taking place. At many companies, IT professionals work hand-in-hand with operations personnel to simulate business processes and help introduce process improvements. Vendors are rapidly innovating products that include document management, workflow, and imaging. The marketplace has realized that technology and business processes are intertwined. The IT professional is in a perfect position to make this seamless web work.

A not-used-nearly-enough software development model may also assist the IT organization in its pursuit of becoming a change agent. Most managers are familiar with the use of prototypes to demonstrate software functionality. Less familiar is the concept of evolutionary software development. Instead of aiming for a complete specification, evolutionary development calls for getting some piece of the solution working in the production environment. The total solution is implemented rapidly via a series of incremental steps or software releases that build on the previous system release. Software maintenance is carried out in a similar fashion. Successful use of this model requires a much more intimate relationship between software designers and developers and the eventual end users. Systems professionals must sit alongside the end users as they develop systems. In this rapidly changing world, processes will constantly be in a state of flux. Therefore, technology support for enhanced processes must be introduced nearly simultaneously. The evolutionary software development model best supports rapid business change, because as processes change, the typical software requirements process will be unnecessary.

The evolutionary software model is in some sense the ultimate antioutsourcing statement. If processes continue to change radically and technology needs to be delivered quickly, there will be no time to send systems development outside. Physical proximity will be advantageous to the process of system developers working closely with end users. How will companies that outsource their information systems be able to make software changes quickly enough in this environment? It will be even more interesting to see how U.S. companies that have outsourced their critical systems development to places such as India or Russia will meet this new pressure on cycle times.

Chief information officers can only become viable change agents when senior corporate management considers them experts in processes, technologies, and organizations. Many companies are forming internal consulting organizations and dedicated business unit–facing groups in which IT can assume the leadership role in creating change and opportunity.

Plumbers and Garbage Collectors

User-programmable software could revolutionize the role of the IT organization. User programmability means that end users will be able to build meaningful applications from reusable software components built by systems developers, or they will use off-the-shelf software with its standard tools to build applications. The most dramatic possible effect is that the control of applications will shift from IT personnel to the end users. Even if this takes place on a wide scale, IT will still have a vital and perhaps more important role.

The IT staff will become like plumbers. Plumbers make sure that the proper pipes are in place to support the appliances and fixtures that will need to be added later. In addition, plumbers fix problems with existing pipes, regardless of whether those problems are a result of normal wear and tear or negligence. In this spirit, IT professionals will shift their focus from application development and end-user support to infrastructure development. The IT infrastructure may consist of data layers, network layers, and software tools that can abstract applications from the nasty issues that hardware, databases, and communication protocols create. At the same time, IT will be responsible for the traditional role of ensuring that the hardware, operating systems, and communications networks remain in working order.

Much of the current thinking on software development stresses reuse. The emphasis has been on IT shops building reusable code fragments or objects. These fragments (or objects) can be reused to develop applications with similar functionality. They are also used when applications are replaced, but a significant amount of functionality from the old application is still needed. To accomplish this, object-oriented design and development is stressed. In simple terms, objects are supposed to represent real-world items, such as customers, orders, and employees. Thus, object-oriented software focuses on the behaviors of objects. However, this software development model still puts the IT group at the center of the application development process. The evolution of reusable software will take us to the creation of software tools that a non-IT person can use to build applications.

Conceptually, users will be able to put application pieces together from high-level abstractions using software tools created specifically for this purpose. These tools will rely heavily on the automatic generation of the code needed to run the application. This software model does not stress reuse; rather, it stresses disposal and recreation. It should be quicker to throw out old systems and build the new without going through the painful specification and design stage. In many respects, this is exactly how Advanced Intelligent Network services work in the telecommunications world. In this environment, IT staff will act as garbage collectors—they will need to ensure that the old applications are disposed of properly, so that they do not pollute the vital technology infrastructure.

Although a burgeoning stock market and the inevitable Year-2000 problem will postpone this reality, it is important for IT professionals to avoid falling into the same trap that the steelworkers did. Not so long ago, steelworkers were large in number and highly paid. As the industry changed due to competition and technology, many steelworkers lost their jobs. Those steelworkers that remain in the flourishing mini-mills of today are still highly paid, but they are getting paid for entirely different skills. Only the steelworkers who made the transition from the shovel to the computer remain. Information technology professionals must make the transition from being programmers and analysts to being business partners and change agents. They need to develop business and communications skills and pay attention to the bottom line.

WHAT DOES THE NEW IT MEAN TO YOU?

Information technology is obviously not going away. Almost every corporate decision now has a technology implication. Globalization, new product options, and even new billing mechanisms all require an upgrade or improvement to a company's existing technology base. And it is obvious that IT needs to, and will, change dramatically. Of course, IT organization changes alone will not make the technology a strategic advantage for a company. The remainder of the business must embark on a journey of change that harmonizes with the changes in IT.

On the Soapbox We All Scream for Technology

Dennis Coleman

Technology enables more people to do more things faster and cheaper. If there's anything the world needs more of, technology must be it. What else can remove all natural constraints from the number, rate, and cost of things people can do to one another?

For management, technology is something modern to manage. For workers, it's something modern to work on. By considering the main components of technology, we can understand better our individual roles. This is the only way for the sum of technology to exceed its parts.

Take hardware. Hardware is everything we can never be. It's fast, powerful, tireless, compact, and reliable.

Hardware tends to be off-white and isn't supposed to make much noise. Really loud hardware is a sign that you've got a problem.

Hardware greatly increases the impact and reach of human accomplishment and depravity and can be controlled by the right combination of plug pulling and software. Software is a highly clever, draconian, and proprietary arrangement of hardware instructions. It generally reflects the insights and attitudes of a group of nerds. Who else could capture and automate raw intelligence, for which a group of MBAs discerns a market need?

Because it originates in someone else's mind, the intersection of what software does and what users want to do is not perfect. Groupware allows entire groups of users to experience imperfection at the same time.

Software systems are like onions. The core software, which does something, is surrounded by shells of interface software. These do less and less as you work your way out, but they do it with increasing user-friendliness.

The onion shells interface with other shells, except for the outermost shell, which interfaces with people, some of whom are clueless. Shells prevent people from interfacing directly with the core software and possibly hurting themselves. Without shells, nothing would protect technology users from the dangers of abstract thinking.

(Continued)

(Continued)

Power users who can't get enough software can apply potent development tools to create as much software as they want. Tool vendors don't have to (and probably wouldn't want to) understand all the things that customers can do with their tools. Tools have their own set of interface shells, and the outermost one enables direct user impact on technology without much effort. That's a situation only more software can remedy.

The abundance of ports, adapters, and communications media allows all kinds of hardware and software to be connected. By deploying enough communication and database servers, the network allows mainframe processing to take place on the desktop. This puts microcomputers everywhere and frees up mainframes to manage them.

The network integrates everybody's input/output (I/O) and transmits the final rollup to HQ, where an armada of IT professionals keeps the network humming. Since the people who acquired or developed the hardware and software are no longer there, this can require system integration, standards compliance, and support services.

That's why system integration requires consultants. Configuring, connecting, implementing, and customizing hardware and software to do things for someone else is not easy. It requires a spec written and revised by people who are also no longer there. Only the Big Six accounting firms have the kind of mental horsepower needed to integrate systems on a big scale. They do this with ancient disciplines involving BPR, computer-aided software engineering (CASE), joint application and development (JAD), and total quality management (TQM). That's not the kind of talent the IT group would tolerate in-house.

Information technology sets the standards for whatever the CIO wants. The CEO tells the CIO that legacy hardware and software will play a major role in the CIO's future. As a result, the current system is defined by sophisticated interim standards, such as "Whatever we have is good enough for now." Future standards are based on information gleaned from conferences, airline magazines, marketing brochures, and hospitality suites.

Support is the source of user manuals, bulletins, and technology updates. If support can't help, a call to the help desk engages a person with access to the same manuals, bulletins, and updates. Hotline support from hardware and software vendors backs up the help desk with people who have original copies of the same manuals, bulletins, and updates. Because of this redundancy, software support costs

(Continued)

(Continued)

money—generally more than suicide hotlines, but less than fantasy-friend hotlines.

Technology isn't hard to grasp. It just requires understanding the convergence of hardware, software, and people.

Source: Dennis Coleman, "On the Soapbox We All Scream for Technology," Upside magazine, (November 1996).

Editor's Note: Dennis Coleman, a consultant based in Half Moon Bay, California, is an occasional contributor to Upside magazine.

Corporate downsizing and cost controls have dismantled the old model in which IT received seemingly unlimited funding for initiatives that were only vaguely understood by business unit counterparts. Today, ferocious competition makes those companies that use IT to its fullest advantage only able to participate in the marketplace. Unfortunately, in most corporations, skeptical business unit managers try to squeeze IT to deliver even vaguer notions of the technological promised land: data warehouses, consolidated billing systems, and information architectures. Although the business climate has changed considerably, many managers have not changed their basic paradigm for managing IT. Without a sweeping commitment from the business units, most companies will resign themselves to outsourcing all IT. They will say that it saves them money, because outsourcers can offer economies of scale. What they won't say is that they merely stopped trying, because they were unable to manage IT, let alone make it a competitive advantage.

In his book, *Post-Capitalist Society,* Peter Drucker examines the shift in the structure of the economic system from capital-based to knowledge-based. Drucker sees the successful companies in the world economy of the twenty-first century being deluged with knowledge workers (i.e., workers who are not only smart, but who want to continually learn); what will separate different companies is how they encourage and mobilize knowledge. Knowledge workers, according to

Drucker, will have to completely overhaul their skills every three to four years. This is an interesting commentary, considering the fact that in spite of the technology revolution that has taken place over the last ten years and that is evolving rapidly in one-year time frames at this point, most managers in U.S. corporations have little more than a remedial knowledge of technology. If the status quo remains, managers who lack technology understanding and skills will not be the next century's knowledge workers.

Fundamentally, this means that for the new IT paradigms to have a chance to be successful, the traditional internal customers of IT need to become educated in technology. Initially, business partnerships will take place when the business units are capable of jointly developing solutions with their counterparts in IT. Just as IT personnel need to understand the business much better to craft better solutions, business unit personnel need to understand what the technology is and how it works, so that cost/benefits and strategic implications are better understood. To rephrase this in management parlance, the business units and IT organizations must develop an intimacy as customers of each other's products and services. This intimacy can only take place when the business units better understand what IT is all about, what it is capable of doing, and why.

Information technology's transition from business partner to change agent will be possible only if IT makes a successful transformation in its capabilities and focus and if senior corporate management believes that this paradigm is one that can work successfully. Information technology personnel must assert themselves as change agents and convince senior management colleagues to consider them in lieu of prestigious management consults or less technology-savvy business unit employees. Corporate management should believe and understand that the talent, intelligence, and focus is available internally to do what it traditionally had relied on business unit insiders to do.

Even more education and knowledge will be required for the business units to support a world in which IT staff become plumbers and garbage collectors. As older employees retire and newer employees take their place, the workforce will be injected with more technology-oriented business people. These new business unit employees will be the ones eventually developing applications. Their more senior bosses will have a whole new set of challenges to face. They will not only need to understand the role of IT in its traditional form as a supplier of products and services, but they also will need to manage a workforce of self-starting technology wizards. In addition, IT and business unit management will need to forge entirely new relationships with software vendors. They will need to force vendors of database management systems, such as Oracle and Sybase, turnkey system providers, such as PeopleSoft, and behemoth software providers, like Microsoft, to meet the functional and support needs of both the business unit application builders and the IT plumbers and garbage collectors. This will require quite a paradigm shift.

The IT organization is being forced to change because of a variety of factors. For a company to successfully incorporate the new IT, business units need to change how they perceive and use the IT organization. They also need to become better educated on the fundamentals of IT. Although these changes are corporate in scope, they must be made individually.

5

Vendors

Vendor management and relationships are among the most important aspects in managing technology. Large companies will have hundreds and sometimes thousands of separate technology vendors. These will range from the individual consultant, operating as a one-person company, to large corporations, such as Microsoft, that may have a presence on every desktop at the company. These vendor relationships must be considered, evaluated, and managed on various fronts. This chapter explores several critical topics related to managing technology vendors successfully including:

- Managing the day-to-day relationships
- Evaluating and identifying which vendors are strategic and how to go approach vendor relationships
- Ensuring that the best prices are achieved
- Understanding the rules of the game regarding outsourcing

As technology expenditures grow and the business becomes even more dependent on technology, vendor relationships cannot be ignored or put off as unimportant. Picking the right partners on the technology can have long-lasting benefits for the firm. Unfortunately, picking the wrong partners can have long-term detrimental effects.

VENDOR RELATIONSHIPS SHOULD NOT BE TAKEN LIGHTLY, AND THE APPROPRIATE RESOURCES NEED TO BE ASSIGNED

If there are hundreds of relationships that companies have on the technology front, there needs to be a systematic way to ensure that they are being managed properly. It is insufficient to have the roll-up-their-sleeves technologists responsible for day-to-day management of key vendor relationships. Countless interactions are required with salespeople, technologists, and vendor management. It is important that these interactions are handled professionally, needs are communicated clearly, and the best interest of the company is always represented. This is a difficult chore for even the best of technologists, who need to have their primary interest in ensuring that the technology works properly and has all the features required. Thus, the best approach is to assign liaisons between your company and these key vendors. Of course, these people will not be the only ones that communicate with the vendor, but they will be responsible—much like an account manager.

The skills required to manage vendor relationships are typically different than technical skills expected by managers in their IT personnel. These skills include:

- Negotiation—Vendor relationships, much like other things in life, are not a case of getting everything you want whenever you ask for it. Thus, like most important relationships, it is critical to ensure that there is an appropriate level of give-and-take. On one extreme, do not be overbearing, expecting to get everything; on the other, ensure that your company's personnel understand how to ask for something. If you do not ask, you rarely will receive.

- Dispute resolution—Critical deliverables are sometimes missed, and service and support is always a challenge for vendors. When disputes arise, it is important that they are quickly resolved to the satisfaction of both companies.

- Interpersonal skills—The people who manage vendor relationships must be approachable and as unbiased as possible. They must be able to communicate what is important and be someone that both sales and technical people from the vendor can relate to.

- Project management to prioritize issues that arise—A balanced, long-term approach to managing vendors requires a person to drive the most important issues, both within the organization and outside. Many critical components of vendor deliverables often rely on tasks that need to be executed by both companies. Sometimes, the vendor needs access to personnel at your company to complete their deliverables. For instance, if computer people at your company are not available to answer questions about the peculiarities of your company's technical environment, vendors may miss crucial deliverables on products that need to be customized. Therefore, the person on the inside must ensure that internal deliverables are met, as well as external ones.

- Presentation skills—Clearly, the person squaring off with the vendor must be able to articulate your company's strategic direction over time. This will ensure that long-term needs are well understood by the vendor. To do this, vendor management needs to encompass presentations to senior people at the vendor company.

 Not all vendor relationships should be treated equally. Do not put too much focus in areas in which the vendor has an insignificant presence, there is little financial investment, or there are no critical business dependencies.

 ## KNOW WHAT A STRATEGIC RELATIONSHIP REALLY IS

There was an article several years ago in *Harvard Business Review* that described how companies such as State Farm and MBNA were particularly successful, because they understood what they wanted (e.g., demographics) from their customers. They built their entire strategy around identifying, procuring, and retaining those customers that fit the business model that they were trying to create. A by-product of this strategy was that some customers were ultimately jettisoned, because they were not profitable, not loyal, or too costly to keep.[1]

The moral of this story applies in several ways as to how companies need to think about forming relationships with key information technology suppliers.

- A company must decide that it, indeed, wants to build strong, long-term relationships with certain suppliers. It should not be something that the company merely stumbles into. This requires homework and diligence.

- It is equally important that the company be an appropriate key customer of the supplier. This parallels the values that MBNA and State Farm bring to the table. Clearly, like most relationships, customer-supplier relationships require mutually beneficial viewpoints other than the mere short-term financial attractiveness.

These two guidelines mentioned above cascade into a multitude of tasks that a company must do to ensure success in building strategic relationships. They can best be characterized as a process for strategic evaluation.

STRATEGIC EVALUATION

Thinking about supplier relationships strategically requires a systematic approach. It is critical that the key technologies be identified over some time horizon (the longer the better, but realistically, 12 to 36 months for most technologies) and then vendors in those areas selected for evaluation. This evaluation should be thought out, documented, and given the exposure to senior managers.

FACTORS TO PICK WINNERS
Service after the Sale

Buying technology is not like buying a carton of eggs or paper clips. As technology grows in complexity and the need to increase the amount of integration between various technologies expands, service after the sale becomes a greater factor in determining which vendors a company should do business with.

Therefore, it is important to understand how a vendor plans to support their products going forward, what types of special service advantages they can bring to this account, what the escalation paths are for problems, and how well they are aligned internally between sales, support, and engineering.

Product Mix Now

This is a rather simple premise but often overlooked. Many times, companies try to pick strategic vendors on some speculative product introduction sometime in the future. If you are involved in R&D or venture capital, this is an appropriate strategy. However, if you are trying to use technology to help your company make money sometime in the near future, this is a faulty premise.

Companies with solid products that fit well with the technology that exists in your company are good fits. The relationship will be better served if one or more of the supplier's products can be used within the next six months. This will build confidence in the relationship and a better willingness to partner in the future.

Product Strategy

It is important to know what is next for the supplier. Sure, they may have a great product now, but we all know how much technology changes. Where are they headed? How much are they investing in new product development? Are they forthcoming in discussing product strategy?

There are no guarantees that a company will pick or develop a winning strategy more than once, but it is a sure sign if they are skimming on details about where they are investing or if they appear to be milking their current product line for all it's worth. Another issue relates to companies that have great products today and a more impressive future direction, but the product that you are interested in is not part of that future.

Company Viability

There is certainly something exciting about working with the new kid on the block. They are often exciting, dynamic, aggressive, and overly helpful. But, would you want to bet the ranch on them? That is the question to ask.

The last thing you need is to tie yourself to a company that is barely surviving or has to sweat to make payroll. If you are really thinking of having a serious strategic relationship with a company, under nondisclosure agreements, they are often more than happy to share financial information. Of course, with public companies, it is only necessary to research Securities and Exchange Commission (SEC) filings and annual reports.

Management

If the management of a company has a proven track record, it greatly increases the chances that the company will be successful. There must be a certain comfort level with the management team—that they understand how important your business is and that they are willing to treat your situation with due diligence.

Start-up firms are not always eliminated from contention simply because they have inexperienced management. In fact, many start-ups will seek out experienced managers to be CEOs, Presidents, and COOs after the exuberance winds down a bit.

Account Management

Is the company willing to put its star performers on your account? If the answer is no, they are probably not ready to have you has a strategic customer. Like most relationships, the day-to-day little things either make or break it. A company that will name the people involved and talk about succession and bench strength will be promising in this regard.

KNOWING HOW AND WHEN TO GET OUT OF KEY RELATIONSHIPS IS AS IMPORTANT TO THE PROCESS AS ENTERING THEM

Strategic relationships need to be reevaluated on a regular basis. Depending on the depth of the commitment and how well things are going, this evaluation can occur as early as six months and no less than once a year. It is at this time that a formal scoring of the vendor should take place along the categories outlined here. If there are danger signs, it is important to do two things. First, schedule a meeting with the management to review your concerns and to try to understand what the vendor's point of view is and what they plan to do to remedy the situation. (Note—regardless of the status of the relationship, it is important to have this review with the vendor.) Second, aggressively seek out alternative vendors, and ensure that the organization is prepared to accept them, both technologically and managerially. So often, companies use technology inappropriately, perform unique customizations, or recruit around a particular technology, making bringing in a new vendor very difficult in a short period of time.

STRATEGIC RELATIONSHIPS CANNOT BE TREATED AS MERE BARTERING RELATIONSHIPS

You cannot nickel-and-dime strategic partners. In technology procurement, like most other things, you tend to get what you pay for. Although you do not want to be ripped off, use your most skillful bullying with those suppliers that you do not care if they walk off. Your key suppliers need to make money off the account, feel good about, and to assign its best staff. Not many companies will be in that position, or can afford it, if they are pounded on to meet constant price demands.

HOW MANY SUPPLIERS SHOULD YOU HAVE?

This is an age-old debate. By limiting the number of suppliers, you usually increase risk, because vendors can come and go, and problems often occur. If you have a wide-open procurement policy based on who is hottest or best price, this is very transaction oriented, it does not give suppliers comfort, and it is difficult to manage.

As we discussed, not all suppliers will be strategic. However, for strategic suppliers, there are some rules of thumb.

- Always have a primary and secondary—Buying from only one supplier should be avoided, because, as mentioned previously, it is not always easy to get out.
- Keep relationships/discussions with two, but no more than four, other companies that operate in the same technology area—This allows for a migration away when it is appropriate, as well

as keeps people in your organization abreast of the marketplace.

OUTSOURCING

For those unfamiliar, the outsourcing concept is similar to what most companies do with services such as cafeterias. Instead of hiring workers internally to do the job, the company contracts with an outside company that specializes in food preparation. For the IT area, outsourcing, according to Gartner Group's definition, is a contractual relationship with an outside vendor to assume responsibility of one or more IT functions. It is usually characterized by the transfer of assets (facilities, staff, hardware) and can include data centers, wide-area networks, application development and maintenance functions, end-user computing, and business processes. Outsourcing has become a critical component of managing technology investment at many companies.

In fact, outsourcing is a burgeoning trend among America's fastest growing companies, according to Coopers & Lybrand's Trendsetter Barometer survey. The February 1997 study reveals that 83 percent of fast-growing firms now use outsourcing; on average, those firms spent just over 9 percent of their 1996 budgets on outsourcing activities. The main reason companies turned to outsourcing, says the report, is money: 63 percent of respondents believe that outsourcers are more efficient or better able to reap economic benefits. For more information on the Coopers & Lybrand Trendsetter Barometer, visit http://www.colybrand.com/eas/trendset/152.html.

At the same time, outsourcing has become a tremendous business opportunity. According to 1997 market figures by Dataquest, worldwide markets for IT professional services will grow from an estimated $158.9 billion in 1996 to approximately $347.7 billion by the year 2001, growing at a compound annual growth rate (CAGR) of 17.0 percent. U.S. markets are estimated to be $73.1 billion in 1996 and will experience a 15.2-percent CAGR for the same period.

Thus, outsourcing is no longer the refuge of the financially weak or technically deficient enterprise, nor is it a stick to threaten an errant IS department. It has become an accepted strategic

Stellar Performer: Allied Signal

James D. Best outlines the various approaches taken by Allied Signal when it comes to managing technology suppliers in his book, *The Digital Organization.*

Like many companies that have thought carefully about this issue, Allied Signal makes every attempt possible to limit the number of suppliers. They use an approach called "Gold, Lead, or Dead." Outside suppliers are ranked on a quality-rating system with attributes such as on-time delivery, quality, price, and after-market support as important factors. Gold suppliers are the most privileged of the bunch. They have the right to bid on all new procurements and can present regularly to key management staff. Lead suppliers are a notch behind. They can bid on deals but must beat a Gold supplier overwhelmingly on technology, price, or both. Finally, products from Dead suppliers are actively being moved out of the organization.

As a way of motivating suppliers, Allied Signal sends letters to salespeople and company executives whenever a supplier moves between tiers. This promotes a system in which it is clear where vendors sit, both internally and externally. Taking it one step further, Allied Signal posts the names of Gold Suppliers in the company reception room for all to see.

Source: James D. Best, The Digital Organization.

Stellar Performer: British Petroleum

In 1993, BP Exploration Operating Co., Ltd., a large division of British Petroleum Co. that explores for and produces oil and gas, outsourced all its information technology operations. This was done in an effort to cut costs, gain more flexible and higher-quality IT resources, and refocus the IT department on activities that would improve the overall business. Although somewhat famous for its plunge into an outsourcing arrangement similar to the alliance concept described below, BP's approach makes it noteworthy on the vendor management front.

BP's solution was to hire three contractors to work together to deliver a single, seamless IT service. To manage the relationships, BP retained 150 people in its IT department. These employees engage in the following activities in managing the relationships:

Scrutinizing actual costs—BP insists on a structure in which the suppliers itemize costs along direct, allocated, and corporate overhead. Because there is an open-book policy with the vendors, BP can review all charges when it sees fit to do so.

Negotiating performance contracts—Each year, BP negotiates performance contracts with the suppliers. They have created a balanced scorecard focused on measuring value to the business to do this. Suppliers receive points for innovation, business process improvement, financial management, customer focus, and organizational learning. Using a formula that sums the points and weights them based on business conditions, BP determines the margins that the suppliers can earn on direct, billed services.

Benchmarking—Although we will discuss benchmarking in detail in Chapter 6, it is important to highlight this as a key activity for BP. BP visits other suppliers of similar services to understand quality and the range of services provided. In addition to working with the existing suppliers, BP has left a contractual opening that allows them to force a vendor to subcontract a service to another company if they have particular quality levels or innovations.

Source: Harvard Business Review *(May-June 1995).*

tool of corporate America. Organizations with benchmark IS operations, such as Xerox Corporation, have taken the plunge. But as with any business practice that has joined the mainstream, there's a danger that decision makers will overlook the pitfalls and take the conventional wisdom of outsourcing for granted. Despite the pervasiveness of outsourcing, megadeals continue to grab headlines: "Major Company X Outsources Whole Shebang to Big Vendor Y for 10 Years and $500 Million!" The volume of these deals ebbs and flows, but they will not be the wave of the future. In reality, selective outsourcing, in which portions of an IT operation are outsourced for shorter time spans, is the standard deal today and will be in the coming years. What to outsource has historically been decided by the question, "Is it strategic to my business?" If the answer is yes, you'd keep it. If no, farm it out. Today, companies are asking a different question: "Is it my core competency?" If no, then it's ripe for outsourcing, whether it's strategic or not. For that reason, organizations are more likely to outsource application development, a function considered sacrosanct just a couple of years ago.[2]

What Is Typically up for Grabs in an Outsourcing Relationship?

- Data center
- Wide-area networks
- Application services, including system development and maintenance
- End-user computing
- Core operating infrastructure (i.e. Windows NT, UNIX)

Why Outsource?

Traditionally, cost reduction has been the overwhelming motivation and perceived payback for outsourcing. Today, cost reduction still tops many priority lists, but the goal of strategic value has grown to rival it. Such value can include new applications, productivity improvement, access to new technology and skill sets, and process or infrastructure redesign. Increasingly, outsourcing is viewed as a bridge solution or reprieve.

Companies outsource IT functions for a number of reasons:

- Achieve marketplace leadership.
- Allow companies to focus on core competencies.
- Establish new IT management models and processes.
- Accommodate changing infrastructures resulting from mergers and acquisitions.
- Convert fixed allocated costs to variable.
- Extend global reach.
- Facilitate best-of-breed implementation of new applications.
- Improve time to market; accelerate reengineering benefits.
- Obtain access to world-class IT capabilities.
- Change IT culture.
- Retain and reskill staff for emerging needs.
- Find skilled IT professionals (the right skill mix).
- Stay on the bleeding edge of technology.
- Convert legacy systems resources to new development.
- Form preferred vendor relationships.
- Optimize IT financial assets.
- Share risk.
- Gain control of difficult-to-manage or out-of-control functions.
- Manage increased diversity of components, heterogeneity.
- Provide asset management of distributed resources.
- Ensure infrastructure reinvestment for critical business functions.

OUTSOURCING CRITERIA

As mentioned above, technology outsourcing is becoming a critical part of how technology is managed throughout the world.

Much has been written on this topic. Below are some key points found in *CIO* magazine that should help the business manager ensure that an outsourcing choice is evaluated properly.[3]

Is the Vendor Capable?

The first thing to determine is whether the vendors vying for your business are truly capable of handling it. Look for the following telltale clues that can make or break an outsourcer's chances:

- How much experience does the vendor have in your industry?

- Will you have to teach the outsourcer the basics of your business, or can you leverage its industry-specific skills?

- Where is the outsourcer making its technology investments?

- How does the vendor treat its people? If you plan on turning over part of your staff to an outsourcer, you want to know what career paths and compensation it will offer. Ask about the retention rate of employees taken in from other outsourcing customers.

- Can the outsourcer absorb your capital investments? If you've spent a lot of money on systems and software, you want to know if the supplier can use at least some of the equipment.

- Is the outsourcer open about what it cannot do? Being up-front about what a company cannot provide is a sign that the company is confident in its abilities in which it says it can provide a service.

Does the Culture Fit?

As you interview vendors and check references, you'll start to get a feel for one of the most important, albeit squishy, aspects of successful outsourcing: *culture fit.* Granted, that area is much akin to the U.S. Supreme Court's definition of obscenity—people can't necessarily define culture fit, but they know it when they see it. Yet, there is a handful of factors you can compare:

- Style: Is your shop a Dockers-and-loafers office and your potential supplier a shirt-and-tie operation? That shouldn't be a deal breaker, but make it a consideration.

- Management: Does the vendor manage its outsourcing teams remotely, or does it keep its management staff on-site? Communication is vital in an outsourcing relationship, and it can make a big difference if vendor managers are easily accessible.

- Problem solving: How do your potential outsourcers handle conflicts that arise in the negotiation process? The way you interact at the negotiation table may foreshadow actual relationship dynamics.

- How well the outsourcers work together: In this era of multivendor alliances, this is another cultural determinant.

What'll This Cost Me?

And then, there's the bottom line. Cost generally is the last factor all parties want to stress in an outsourcing relationship, but ultimately, it is the only one that is quantifiable. Three areas to focus on are:

- Price variability: Variability is what you want in a pricing structure. Rather than the fixed costs of maintaining current investments, say, in legacy systems and staff, you want a sliding, pay-as-you-go structure.

- Flexibility: Ensure that when your IT environment changes, your vendor can accommodate the change with minimal fuss or restructuring of costs.

- Shared risk: Agreements that are tied to service levels for the organization or that ensure that certain staff is assigned from the outsourcer shows that the outsourcer is putting more than a little skin in the game.

 Beware of the low-ball bid. The low price today isn't always the best value tomorrow. When you look at a vendor's projected costs, watch for hidden costs—for services that aren't covered in the contract—and consider how they'll escalate during the life of the agreement. In actuality, there is often a world of difference between a vendor's quoted price and the ultimate bill. For example, if you're offered a 25-percent reduction in data center costs, that figure may not include additional markups for overhead expenses or profit margin.

The good news about cost is that your final couple of prospects will probably be pretty similar in their pricing. That will free you to focus on softer aspects of the deal, such as culture fit. When you

Stellar Performer:
AT&T Human Resources

To help manage its IS workload, AT&T Human Resources (HR) turned to Keane, Inc., an outsourcing firm based in Boston, to help maintain a portfolio of 26 legacy applications. According to the terms of the $11 million fixed-price contract, Keane assumed responsibility for changes and enhancements to the 26 applications. In addition to freeing AT&T's staff to concentrate on application development, the outsourcing deal has had another huge benefit: AT&T estimates that it has saved over $1 million so far.

Service contracts for application maintenance can help IT departments better identify their costs as a starting point for managing and containing those costs. AT&T HR's maintenance agreement with Keane shows the power that such arrangements can offer IT departments that are searching for ways to stretch their budgets. AT&T still pays for end-user service through its contract with Keane. But now it bills end users directly for the services they request. The arrangement has worked out so well that AT&T HR recently outsourced seven more applications to Keane, whose efficient economies of scale required the addition of just two more employees to service the additional applications.

The maintenance contract enables AT&T HR to "justify the benefit they received for every dollar spent," asserts Brian Keane, senior vice president for Keane's IS division. Such information can be a powerful ally for IS departments when top management acts to reduce budgets. When faced with such edicts or requests, IT management can talk specifically about what requests and what the impact will be. Thanks to its outsourcing deal with Keane, AT&T HR management now reports that its applications are running better. Keane has streamlined modules, reduced the number of help calls, and produced miscellaneous code improvements.

Source: Datamation *(June 1997).*

tally up those points, it won't be hard to spot the winner.

KEY CONCEPT — OUTSOURCING ALLIANCES

The latest wrinkle in outsourcing is the so-called alliance contracts. Instead of a company signing a deal with one firm to manage the entire business or to do spot deals with niche suppliers, companies are selecting a few firms for major areas and keeping quite a bit themselves as well. Companies such as DuPont who recently formed an alliance with Computer Sciences Corp. and Andersen Consulting are looking for variability and flexibility in the IT services and solutions available to all the businesses within the organization.

Today, the challenge for any company seeking IT partners is to figure out a way to preserve and enhance its internal IS organization. Internal IT organizations typically have accumulated industry knowledge and expertise that a company cannot afford to lose. When thinking about forming an alliance, the IT organization itself needs to focus on growth and diversification—ensuring access to leading-edge technologies, broadening the career opportunities for its people, and providing for competitive economies at affordable costs for its operating units.

For instance, DuPont is creating a virtual IT organization that takes the strengths of its two partners and blends them with DuPont's knowledge of its industry. DuPont retains a large IT operation and the team that will lead and manage the alliance. CSC will provide global IT services—maintaining data centers, networks, distributed computing, and generic applications—at DuPont's Wilmington, Delaware, headquarters and at various plant sites. Andersen provides chemical business solutions designed to improve manufacturing, marketing, distribution, and customer service.

Among the major benefits that organizations can expect to realize from such an alliance:

- Increased flexibility and speed, both from a variable cost standpoint and in delivering business solutions
- Access to new technologies and skills

- Work elimination through differentiated and/or reduced service levels
- Ongoing productivity improvement
- Operational reliability and infrastructure renewal
- Enhanced training and development opportunities for IT employees[4]

THE RECENT BACKLASH AGAINST TECHNOLOGY OUTSOURCING

Although outsourcing has been a strategic initiative for many companies over the last few years, several companies that used this strategy are finding problems with this approach. There are a variety of reasons for problems. In essence, the reason for most perceived problems is missed expectations by the vendors providing services.

At the forefront, one of the main areas in which outsourcing can disappoint is in the cost reduction it delivers. As long ago as 1995, Deloitte & Touche, having conducted a survey of 1,500 CIOs in the United States and Canada, showed that only 31 percent believed that their outsourcing cost savings were significant. Sixty-nine percent were disappointed (Figure 5.1).

Customers believe outsourcers, with their economies of scale and superior resources, can do IT much more cheaply than internal staffs. Many business leaders anticipate 30- to 50-percent savings. In reality, such savings are rare. In addition, many contracts don't reflect changing market pricing. Market costs for hardware, software, and personnel dip over time, but fixed-price-outsourcing deals stay level.

Another problem is that outsourcers need to subcontract to find key personnel. Thus, companies that outsource are often unpleasantly surprised to find that their vendor isn't working on their projects—somebody else is. Customers complain that vendors aren't up-front about this and that subcontractors, unfamiliar with contract provisions and customer expectations, don't always deliver the required service in the expected way. One safeguard is to build subcontractor approval rights into contracts and to specify that key, mission-critical projects or systems be handled only by the primary vendor.

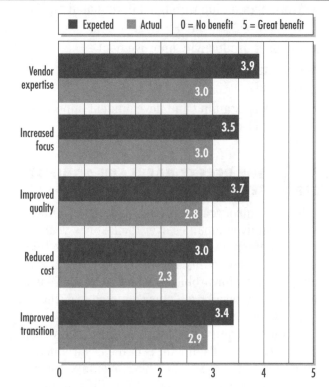

FIGURE 5.1 *Deloitte & Touche Consulting Group Survey of 488 Companies*[6]

Another key pitfall, and one to which ten-year deals are highly susceptible, is scope shift. Business needs change from year to year, let alone decade to decade. It's impossible to anticipate needs several years out when negotiating an agreement. Customers can find themselves butting heads with their vendors a few years into the deal, wishing they had defined change management procedures or built flexibility amendments into the contract. A logical solution might be simply to pursue shorter-term deals, but the major vendors seem to favor longer contracts and talk customers into signing on for longer hitches than they originally intended. Fortunately, today there are more ways to terminate a contract, but it's still difficult to do. Vendor liability is limited; if the outsourcer fails to perform, the customer will have trouble collecting on its losses. Above all, there is still a lot of contract ambiguity in defining services and how they are to be provided. That can come back to haunt customers when the vendor answers a request with, "Sorry, it's not in the contract."[5]

In the same Deloitte & Touche survey, it was found that 53 percent of the companies that outsourced have renegotiated their contracts, and 8 percent brought the technology back in house. Another 16 percent of those that renegotiated ended up turning to a different vendor.

 Outsourcing is not always cheaper or easier, as evidenced by the recent backlash. There has been quite a bit written about this topic from survey information to case studies. The point is that not all software developers are equal; there is additional management and diligence time required to manage the relationship with the outsourcer; and over time, many rates of outsourcers increase.

Some Companies Have Abandoned Outsourcing

Recently, several companies have discontinued their outsourcing contracts. In May 1997, less than halfway through its seven-year term, MONY, the New York insurer, terminated its $210 million contract with outsourcer Computer Sciences Corporation. The management of MONY spent the next six months rebuilding its internal team. LSI Logic cut short a five-year deal with IBM Global Services. "The linkage between technology and business processes is so tight that when you outsource, somehow you get dysfunctional," says Lam Truong, CIO.[7] Southern New England Telephone canceled a desktop support contract with I-Net less than a year after it was signed because of negative cultural impact on end users. The end users were against calling a toll-free number for services, despite the cost savings.

6

Best Practices in Technology Management

Throughout this book, we have established how important IT has become in business. In many instances, it has grown from a means to an end to an end in itself in some cases. Industries use and develop technologies in many different ways, customizing systems for their own processes and products. In addition, no different from other things in business (such as working capital or human resources), companies simply are unable to use technology with the same effectiveness.

This chapter examines issues relating to the use of technology across a broad spectrum of companies and industries, including:

- What techniques can be used to help your company be a leading user of technology?
- Best use of IT in manufacturing companies.
- Technology implementations that are giving companies strategic advantage.

BENCHMARK BEST PRACTICES IN TECHNOLOGY MANAGEMENT

It is never easy to learn without role models. In most instances, people develop skills and techniques by watching and finding out what others do. People copy the good things, modify them a little for their unique needs or to fit their personalities, and discard the things that they do not find useful. Benchmarking is a technique that is used to structure how one company can learn successful organization from another. Companies use benchmarking to learn what other companies are doing on business processes that are important to them. Although the general approach needs to be adapted to fit into the appropriate or most effective use of IT, the general premise of benchmarking—to learn from others—still has much validity.

A GENERAL DISCUSSION OF BENCHMARKING

Before benchmarking became a distinct approach to organizational improvement, it was just a shrug of common sense. Of course, the best way to learn is by watching others. The legendary Henry Ford, for example, gleaned tips for his car assembly line by observing production methods in a Chicago slaughterhouse. Way back then, the unsophisticated probably just called it a good idea. In the 1980s, Big Business dressed it up and gave it a good haircut and a catchy name. As is the case with all buzzwords, the handle now stands in for the idea it was coined to describe.

As benchmarking has progressed from fad to fixture, the preoccupation with its practice, rather than the reasons it should (or shouldn't) be done, and how to apply what is learned has led many companies to an everybody-else-is-doing-it-and-so-should-we mentality. For others, it has become a substitute for in-depth thinking about their business and goals: I benchmark, therefore, I must have a strategic clue.

That perspective has been aided by the emphasis that competitions, most notably the Malcolm Baldrige National Quality Award, put on doing and measuring instead of learning. According to the American Productivity & Quality Center's International Benchmarking Clearinghouse (IBC), 55 percent of the criteria for the Baldrige Award relate to benchmarking and best practices.

Benchmarking is implemented in a variety of ways. But depending on whether it is outsourced or coupled with other initiatives, the basic routine works like this: A company identifies the processes that are central to its business and then selects the top-performing companies in those areas. By analyzing how that excellence is achieved, the company learns lessons that it can apply to its own processes.

Benchmarking can deliver significant performance improvements and returns based on efficiency, cost savings, and new revenues. Benchmarking projects typically target cycle times, productivity, customer service, quality, and production costs. They also can be part of an effort to shift the culture of a company to be more customer-oriented and results-focused.

Many companies make the mistake of letting the benchmarking process become an end in itself. This is most common in corporate settings in which special full-time benchmarking teams are established, says Eileen C. Shapiro, author of *Fad Surfing in the Boardroom: Reclaiming the Courage to Manage in the Age of Instant Answers.* "You end up with these people who travel to the most fascinating countries and companies and know all sorts of stuff, and there is absolutely no way to figure out how this knowledge applies to their own company," Shapiro says. "You really just create this elite club of frequent flyers."[1]

Getting lost in the process obscures the point of benchmarking, which is performance improvement. For example, Florida Power & Light Company received the Deming Prize in 1989 for its benchmarking excellence. Later that same year, a new CEO came in and dismantled large portions of the company, because its structure was geared toward excessive benchmarking. "He found the company was more committed to winning awards than serving the customer," says Alan Weiss, president of Summit Consulting, Inc., in East Greenwich, Rhode Island, and author of *Our Emperors Have No Clothes* (Career Press, Inc., 1995). That kind of loss of focus is less likely to occur if benchmarking is an integral part of the jobs of line managers, who have other responsibilities and are more inclined to seek practical applications.

Companies can become preoccupied with the measure, whether it's a satisfaction rating or time-to-market statistic, rather than paying attention to the processes that produce those metrics. The goal becomes not to improve process but to match the best practices at any cost.

The key element in benchmarking is the *adaptation* of a best practice to tailor it to a company's needs and culture. Without that step, a company merely apes another company's process. "What happens with these fads is that people get lazy," Shapiro says. "Instead of saying, 'Federal Express is a brilliant company; let's understand better what they do and build on it and figure out whether it applies to us,' they say, 'Let's try to be Federal Express.' It's a monkey-see, monkey-do kind of thing." This approach condemns benchmarking to fail, because many best practices are as much a function of a company's culture and unique characteristics as they are of process.

Benchmarking can become an undue burden on staff time and company resources. Although return on investment is not the only goal of benchmarking, only one-half of the top benchmarking companies surveyed by the IBC keep track of their financial results. Some companies tout returns in the millions, but it is unclear how consistently benchmarking delivers on this count.

Companies often waste time benchmarking noncritical functions or struggling to raise the performance bar an insignificant amount. Does it really matter to your customers if you shrink your delivery time by two days? If you deliver packages, yes. If you deliver antiques, maybe not. And how much does it cost to cut out those days?[2]

 **GET THE MOST OUT OF IT BENCHMARKING**

Generally, the point of benchmarking companies is to find out more about how successful companies manage specific processes (i.e., order fulfillment, purchasing). The general practice, however, needs to be modified for the purpose of IT. In the case of IT, there are three special aspects that need to be considered.

How IT Departments Operate in Terms of Procedures and Processes

Information technology departments have their own processes that are sometimes interrelated with the remainder of the company's activities and other times not. For instance, the business of IT includes application development, infrastructure deployment, and end-user support. In addition, there are management and financial processes that IT shares as processes with the remainder of the company.

When benchmarking with external IT organizations, it is important to understand how these companies facilitate critical IT business processes. Business unit alignment for applications development, procurement, deployment, and support need to be near the top of the list when trying to find best-of-breed companies.

How Companies Use Specific Technologies to Enable Business Processes

Although much can be learned from benchmarking organizations from any industry, it is important to benchmark within industry to best understand how other IT initiatives enable key business processes.

How IT Groups Implement Technologies and Manage Their End-to-End Life Cycle

Considering the goal of continuously improving IT cost/performance, quality, and effectiveness, while avoiding inappropriate or inefficient IT alternatives, it is critical for IT departments to benchmark with other technology groups at a numerical level. This goes from trying to find the best company with expertise in a specific area to comparing numbers and statistics. Numbers of transactions, support people per one hundred processors, and the amount of overall data at the company are all relevant statistics when trying to compare cost and efficiency across companies. As these numbers are shared and compared, companies can engage in conversations about specific technology choices and where those choices are in their life cycle. From this, a company can learn about inefficient processes and improper technology selections, or it can gain insight into the important decisions that need to be made to incorporate new technologies.

 BEST PRACTICES FOR TECHNOLOGY ORGANIZATIONS

Some technology organizations are better than others. For a given industry, certain types of technological implementation will produce cost savings or strategic advantage. However, it is often difficult to figure out whether the technology group at your firm is doing all of the right things. Although there is no cookie-cutter solution for being great, there are some common traits that leading technology organizations have. The following list illustrates some of the themes that the best try to focus on.

- Developing and obtaining top management commitment to information and IT strategies focused on gaining strategic advantage—Fundamentally, the best IT organizations are linked to the top management of the company. Information technology is not a cost to be contained; rather, it is a part of the overall strategy of the company. The CIO will, most likely, report to the CEO, and the participation in IT decisions will be at the operating board level of the company.

- More extensive cross-functional reorganization of processes affected by IT—As will be elaborated on in a late chapter, IT organizations can take on the role of change agents for a company. In this case, they will not just be providers of technology solutions that the business needs, but, instead, they will be intimately involved in redefining the business processes using technology.

- Expanded user and customer involvement in all aspects of the design and implementation of IT projects—Wherever IT makes a go of it alone, there are usually problems. Joint planning, decision making, and ownership of technology projects is found in the most successful companies.

- Improved customer-driven measures of quality of technology deliverables—Formalizing the success of IT projects can be extremely beneficial for improving and explaining the value that IT has for the business. Service level agreements for availability and outage times are examples of concrete measurements. Structured surveys after large implementations is another.

- Compressing project scope and payback time— To gain a competitive advantage, all companies are trying to do things better, cheaper, and faster. Information technology organizations must take the same approach. Large projects with long-term gains are replaced with smaller projects with a much quicker payback. With the level of innovation going on in the technology market today, IT organizations are forced to rapidly deploy solutions as they become available.

- Post project audits—Learning from one's own mistakes and successes is typically done only in an ad hoc fashion. Structured audits after projects are completed or cancelled help to bring the learning process to a new level. These audits should include project members, business unit customers, and outsiders.

- Benchmarking against outside providers and companies—As was discussed at length earlier in this chapter, benchmarking of outsiders' processes and technologies is imperative to heighten awareness and structure organizational learning. In addition, with outsourcing on the climb, it is necessary for companies to look at how service providers execute on IT initiatives. There are very legitimate reasons to keep IT in house. However, IT organizations that truly know how they compare with outside service companies are one step ahead.

GOING FOR THE BIG BANG OR INCREMENTAL SYSTEMS DEPLOYMENT

Many systems people are inclined to go for a holistic replacement or implementation of a system rather than a phased approach. The beauty in this is that the implementation is less messy and purer—the refreshing "out with the old and in with the new." Unfortunately, this approach often results in failure. These failures occur for many reasons: the project takes too long, management support diminishes, sponsorship disappears, the business need evolved, requirements are difficult to pin down, and so on.

A more pragmatic approach is to develop large systems in *waves* or stages. The implementation should be broken down so that business benefits are delivered early and fairly often. This allows the project to build appropriate momentum while fending off the likely cynicism that takes place when new things are attempted.

For a differing view, however, check out the case study on Quantum provided later in this chapter.

HOW A MANUFACTURING COMPANY SHOULD APPROACH TECHNOLOGICAL INVESTMENT

The manufacturing industry, because it started at the industrial revolution, was perhaps the first to look at things technologically. Rudimentary technologies before the creation of computers, such as time-and-motion studies and assembly line production, were used to mass-produce goods in a cost-effective manner. More recently, it is through technology that the terms of competition have been set in building better cars, stereos, and personal computers. In this chapter, we explore the ins and outs of the latest trends for using technology in the manufacturing setting.

In a study by Theodore Kinni of the best manufacturing plants, he summarizes the four lessons to be learned by manufacturing companies in deploying IT. These lessons are almost like a hierarchy from basic to sophisticated.

1. Use technology to support the business. This fundamental point is sometimes missed. If the IT is not supporting quality, productivity, and agility, then it is probably misused.

2. Create information flows between people. Leading firms connect workers, suppliers, and customers with near real-time information via communication networks. It is not merely the connection between these parties, but the ability to collaborate that makes these networks useful.

3. Integrate production with the use of information systems. Within the factory, leading firms are able to create networks, so that production information is used for real-time measurement, communication, and response.

4. Deploy technology for strategic advantage. This is done either by figuring out what innovations can be made by using technology to develop breakthrough products or by using the technology to gain advantage by industry leading the operational improvements.[3]

Stellar Performer: Quantum

Quantum, a computer hard disk manufacturer with over $4 billion in annual revenue, successfully pulled off a *big bang* implementation, proving that it could be done. After deliberately shutting down their systems for eight days in 1996, Quantum cut over 750 users in 25 locations to a new suite of systems. The systems have been functioning ever since.

Quantum felt that this type of implementation was necessary to fend off potential business threats and to gain a competitive advantage. The new system focused on several areas, including sales processing, inventory, and logistics. It was the critical integration of these functions that Quantum desired, and they could not cope with a piecemeal approach.

So, how and why were they successful? Quantum implemented lofty goals that many companies aspire to, including cross-functional teams, extensive testing and training, supportive management, and good company culture. In addition, a very notable point was the extreme commitment of the business units in seeing the project through to the end.

Source: CIO *magazine (15 February 1997).*

BEST PRACTICES OF THE FUTURE— KNOWLEDGE MANAGEMENT

Taking advantage of the fact that the CIO is getting a more critical role in the corporate planning process and that IT has moved away from the means to gain automation, the next bastion for IT added value may be the elusive category of thinking called knowledge management. The best companies will use IT as part of the process of managing knowledge in the company. So, how will this be done, and what will be the factors? Henry Lasker and David Norton examined corporate knowledge management in an article titled *The New CIO/CEO Partnership.*

Lasker and Norton noted that organizations get better by improving their ability to do new things or old things better. Thus, organizations improve performance by learning how to do things on the basis of accumulated knowledge.

According to Lasker and Norton, managing knowledge and learning is based on three principles. Each of these principles can be heavily assisted by IT.

- Alignment—The knowledge creation process of your organization must link to business strategy or the performance that pushes that strategy.

- Forward thinking—Improving performance means developing new core competencies that do not exist inside the company today but must be learned.

- Communication—Learning is a social activity, and reaching new performance levels requires greater communication across the organization.

Lead technology managers are in a position to play a critical role. Because the infrastructure to develop knowledge management mostly exists in the form of servers and networks, the technology leaders will not need to fight for much capital to help this process move along. Therefore, only a small amount of the IT budget is required, estimated to be no more than 5 percent, note Lasker and Norton.

One such resource shift involves creating user-friendly interfaces that encourage employees to share information across the network (as we are seeing today in the form of browsers and discussion groups). By formalizing the collection and dissemination of information, a company can develop a process for learning. Captured information might include such things as changes in customer strategies, rumors of a new competitor in the market, or a trade press article describing a new regulatory threat.

However, technology managers need to win the respect and cooperation of senior managers at the corporate level. Often perceived as a latecomer to the game and sometimes more concerned with the machinations of the computer than the business, the technology managers must defend ideas for planning and implementing an enterprise-wide knowledge management strategy. At the head of the organization, the CIO must convince his peers and the CEO that he alone is in a position to ensure that the system works across the entire enterprise and is capable of growing and adapting.

However, the CIO must recognize that the IT department cannot control the knowledge infrastructure. Instead, he should set his sights on becoming a senior partner in the knowledge management process. The CIO's role is to build the infrastructure and to develop the interfaces that support the free flow of knowledge. If he embraces the opportunity, he will earn a place in the huddle. If he resists, the IT department is destined to play a supporting, rather than a strategic, role in the company's future.

 KEY TECHNOLOGIES FOR MANUFACTURING INDUSTRIES

Success in the manufacturing industry depends on being able to respond quickly, accurately, and consistently to the changing needs of the marketplace. Successful companies are able to control and optimize processes to vary the necessary parameters to obtain the best product on time and on specification.

Like most industries, there has been a technological shift away from exclusive mainframe computing to a more distributed approach. The distributed systems that assist manufacturing companies perform tasks ranging from shopfloor scheduling and process optimization to material and manufacturing resource planning. At the high end, some systems support finance and strategic planning.

Stellar Performer:
CIGNA

In their article, Lasker and Norton identified CIGNA Property & Casualty as a company that attempts to effectively manage knowledge throughout the company. For CIGNA, like any company, getting people to share information willingly is one of the most difficult aspects of knowledge management. Tom Valerio, senior vice president of transformation at CIGNA, says, "You have to create an upward spiral for know-how to be shared."

At CIGNA, an upward spiral is the mechanism for disseminating knowledge throughout the company. Information is contributed by employees and then processed by *knowledge editors*. The knowledge editors are experienced underwriters and other senior officials. After receiving information from the employee population, it is up to the knowledge editors to distribute it across the organization. For instance, senior underwriters might gather data from the field offices and broadcast relevant information to associates and superiors over CIGNA's internal network.

The company found that the quantity of information was not the key determinant of profitable underwriting. Rather, it was the quality of the information. "Every company has a ton of information in its databases," Valerio notes. "The key to profitable underwriting isn't giving access to every bit of information that's important; it's how you determine which information is relevant and how you tailor it."

Further, CIGNA uses knowledge management to discover and maintain profitable market niches. The skills and experience of its people in underwriting and claims have become the building blocks for new business opportunities. Their knowledge is being used to determine which niches to enter and to what extent.

The IT department has been important to CIGNA's transformation. The company has a CIO for the corporate entity, and each division has a head information systems officer. The head of information systems of the property and casualty unit was a participating member on the executive steering committee that managed the major project initiatives, and staff was involved directly in the knowledge management initiatives.

In addition, the information systems group sponsored the technology for each of the company's three major initiatives: producer relations, underwriting, and claims management. The CIO reviewed the ways technology was being used in each of these three areas.

Source: ComputerWorld *(22 January 1996).*

Inside the plant, there are a few critical technologies that are necessary. These include:

- Programmable logic controllers (PLCs)—A generic term applied to a class of industrial-grade proprietary computers that perform logic functions. They typically replace electro-mechanical and solid-state logic.

- Distributed control systems (DCSs)—A digital, network-based, general-purpose system capable of being configured to control the many loops in an industrial process. They usually have some type of operator interface.

- Man-machine interfaces (MMIs)—Computer systems that allow operators to control and query factory manufacturing systems.

- Supervisory control and data acquisition (SCADA) systems—Systems that enable the process of looking at current activity from a distance, passing operating directives to the remotely located controllers in a factory, and obtaining information from the remote devices.

- Manufacturing execution systems (MESs)—Industrial software for the shopfloor that is generally spoken about as an integrated system that looks at manufacturing operations and integrates the real-time data with production control and distributed control systems.

KEY CONCEPT — SUPPLY CHAIN MANAGEMENT

Supply chain management refers to managing the complex interactions involved in the flow of product across the supply chain—from raw materials procurement, through manufacturing and distribution, to delivery as finished goods to consumers.

Our Manugistics software and services integrate planning activities for product demand, distribution, manufacturing, and transportation across the entire supply chain—not only within a single enterprise, but also among different enterprises along the supply chain. Our clients are using supply chain management to help reengineer their businesses and integrate their supply chains at the operational level. As a result, these companies can make better decisions and achieve enhanced productivity, greater competitive advantage, and improved profitability.

Stellar Performer:
Babcock & Wilcox

Babcock & Wilcox, in Lynchburg, Virginia, uses chemical vapor deposition (CVD) techniques for government and commercial customers. Babcock & Wilcox CIM Systems and Services division implemented a SCADA system developed for another Babcock & Wilcox facility that manufactures nuclear fuels and related products for government and commercial applications, a highly sensitive field with strict security requirements. "Our challenge was to convert manual controls, gas-flow meters, and controllers into an automated system to apply finishes on product surfaces," said Ed Stubbs, automation engineer with the CIM Systems group. "Involved in the project were two fluidized bed furnaces that had been designed for manual control of the temperature, soak time, gas volume, and recipes for multiple-process gases used in CVD. These are large furnaces involving large-scale operations, and operating them manually was inefficient. We knew that automating the systems was a priority to maintain quality and consistency."

Source: Adapted from a White Paper at www.microsoft.com.

Stellar Performer:
Mobil Oil Corporation

Mobil Oil's South Belridge oil field in southern California yields 50,000 barrels of oil each day from 750 producing wells. But just six years ago, it produced only 35,000 barrels a day. Mobil Oil achieved this dramatic production increase by creating an enhanced oil recovery (EOR) process that injects steam into the ground to sweep the oil toward the wells.

Twenty-four hours a day, 365 days a year, the oil wells steadily harvest their reserves. And with the help of its EOR process, the South Belridge lease now produces approximately $500,000 worth of oil a day, leading all domestic Mobil Oil production. But EOR is expensive, requiring a lot of above-ground facilities to make the oil recovery possible. "The oil is what makes us the money," said Mobil LAN Administrator, Bill Bissett. "All the other facilities are required to do business. Obviously, we need to control those nonrevenue-producing costs as much as possible."

To control costs, Mobil installed an MMI system that linked the site's existing network of 319 PLCs to 22 off-the-shelf 486-PCs. The MMI system now monitors and controls more than 30,000 data points throughout the operation. Most workstations are in the field, but five terminals are located in the office and operate as data concentrators and flow control managers. Operators use these workstations to adjust oil, steam, electricity, and other variables to meet specified cost targets. "For example, instead of going out to 50 steam generators, looking at the pressures, and adjusting each one manually, we now adjust all the pressures from a single PC here in the office," said E. D. Neilands, a senior staff electrical engineer at the site.

Source: Adapted from a White Paper at www.microsoft.com.

Manugistics pioneered the development of integrated supply chain management software and, for more than a decade, has been helping clients define and implement successful supply chain management solutions. Headquartered in Rockville, Maryland, the company has offices worldwide.

Here is an example of how the software is used by Reynolds. Customer and product purchase history information is combined via a demand-planning module in the software. This software then keeps close tabs on the projected sales of many of Reynolds's packaging products. Then, using another component of the software that has transparency into manufacturing capacity, users at Reynolds can determine the optimum balance between customer demand and inventory levels.

All this success, however, does not come without some fits. There is certainly a mind-set, as well as a business process change, required to take advantage of the software in an optimal manner. This requires users to trust a system in addition to an integrated collection of manufacturing, sales, and customer data in a single place. Reynolds's ability to fight through some of these challenges shows how a technology, although still in its infancy, can be used to make a significant difference in company performance.

THE USE OF TECHNOLOGY TO SUPPORT INVENTORY MANAGEMENT

Inventory management systems instantaneously record every product movement in and out of your warehouse. These systems are essential for key decisions that ultimately effect the bottom line. Properly understanding and determining inventory directly equates to return on investment, especially considering that warehouse costs and returns are so expensive.

The key metrics that an inventory management system can help collect include:

- Inventory turnover—An effective inventory-tracking system can tell a CEO how often every product in inventory is used and replaced. An efficiently managed inventory turns over as frequently as possible to minimize the amount of cash that is tied up in the warehouse. Order

Stellar Performer:
Solectron Corporation

With 7,000 employees worldwide, Solectron Corporation is a major supplier of circuit boards and electronic assemblies for companies such as IBM Corporation, Hewlett-Packard Company, and Intel Corporation. It has manufacturing facilities in California, Washington, Malaysia, France, and Scotland, and it has an office in Japan. Initially, each facility acted independently in its automation projects, because it was so hard to provide data access to them all. The only linking was done by people moving information between locations. There was no way to pull results into a common database or to track circuit board assemblies across divisions. As a result, managers weren't getting the high level of information needed to monitor the shop floor, and customers weren't getting the information they needed in a timely manner.

Solectron needed a scalable, enterprise-wide information system in which developing and integrating new applications would be quick and easy. The first application was a Shopfloor-Tracking and Recording System (STARS), which allows workers to record the movement of circuit boards through the assembly and testing processes. Bar code readers capture and enter subassembly information, test results, quality information, and a variety of other data directly into the STARS application. Customers can access information about their work remotely so they know the status of each job. Another application is a worldwide materials database, using EDI servers.

Source: Adapted from a White Paper at www.microsoft.com.

Stellar Performer: Reynolds Metals Company

Reynolds Metals Company, producer of the favorite kitchen item, Reynolds Wrap, was looking into improving its forecasting for production. With thousands of products and millions of dollars of inventory, the forecasting of sales demand not only could lead to the decline of overproducing, but a mere 1-percent improvement was deemed to represent millions of dollars of savings to the bottom line.

The goal was set by CEO Jeremiah Sheehan to reduce internal inventories by $100 million annually. To accomplish this goal, Reynolds set out on deploying supply chain–planning software. Within a year of the deployment of the software, Reynolds had cut overall forecasting errors from 15 percent to as little as 5 percent. In addition, an important by-product has been the increase in customer satisfaction by meeting the demands of short lead times.

Source: Information Week *(16 June 1997).*

cycles vary by company; however, manufacturers' inventories by product line should turn over six to eight times a year.

- Percentage of orders shipped on time—As much of a profitable business practice as it is, there is a risk attached to quick inventory turnover. Companies with excellent inventory may have problems filling orders as quickly as customers require. Thus, it is important to track the percentage of orders shipped on time via the inventory management system. If the percentage falls below the mid-90s, inventory levels probably should be raised.

- Length of time to fill back orders—Running hand in hand with percentage of orders shipped on time is the ability to fill back orders quickly. By examining back orders in the inventory management system, a company can get a good idea for the products that need an increase in production and warehousing.

- Percentage of customer complaints to shipped orders—Although not typically integrated with the inventory management system, it is critical to examine customer complaints in relation to the inventory and warehousing. In terms of inventory management, examining the complaints that are related to late orders or missed back-order dates will help guide the appropriate levels of product needed in the warehouse. Although looking at the raw data is very helpful, it is the relation to actual complaints that often points to the most important issues from a customer perspective.

USE SCANNING TECHNOLOGY AND WIRELESS CONNECTIONS TO IMPROVE OPERATIONS

We are all familiar (although George Bush wasn't) with the scanners at the grocery store that are used to get prices for the goods purchased. They were put in place to speed lines and to reduce the errors of manual input. The same type of technology is available for use in a variety of industries. At the same time, this technology is much more mobile than it once was, so it can be put to very clever uses. A typical use is a scanner or mobile computer that has an antenna that beams signals to receivers on the ceiling. These signals are captured, the data is processed, and it is sent to central computers for storage.

At manufacturing plants, hand-held scanners are enabled by wireless connections to computers, allowing for seamless materials management, quality control inspections, and product tracking. For example, an employee would wave the scanner over the bar-coded goods and input a few pieces of data about their quality. This information would go to a central computer, and it could be used to ensure that the manufacturing process is producing the level of quality required.

In warehouses, this type of technology helps provide instant accountability on tens of thousands of items. With every transaction (a sale, a movement, or a return), a main database can be continually updated. This allows for much smoother inventory management, as well as customer satisfaction, because cycle times can be radically reduced.

As mentioned above, the grocery store example is well known. An emerging use is in other facets of the retail industry. For instance, at large department stores, scanning technology can be used for point-of-sale information, product placement in the store, and to ensure that inventory is properly managed.

CALL CENTER TECHNOLOGY IS CRITICAL TO CUSTOMER SATISFACTION AND SALES

Customer satisfaction is extremely important in today's competitive environment. In many service industries, customers are encouraged to buy products, lodge complaints, and ask questions via telephone to far-flung call centers. Even as the Internet emerges as a way of conducting business, the fast-and-true 800-service will still be a critical component to many sales and marketing strategies. Having said that, customers do not want to wait for agents to pick up the telephone or to be delayed in receiving information once they are speaking to an agent. At the same time, outbound calls from telemarketing centers are used by many sales organizations to have an expansive reach to spread out customer bases.

To increase efficiency, improve sales, and win back customers, companies are investing in call

Stellar Performer:
Bell Canada

To compete in the newly deregulated environment, Bell Canada needed to focus on customer retention and win-back. To assist in this effort, they installed a sophisticated call center system to help agents engaged in telemarketing. The role of the telemarketers was to blitz the landscape with the promise of reduced prices. The outcome was to be either increased customer retention or gaining back early defectors.

The technology that Bell Canada deployed relies on advanced calling technology to dial through long lists of prospects for long-distance services. Busy signals, no-answers, and answering machines are filtered out in one-fiftieth of a second, and only live calls are transferred to the telephone agent where follow-up can be conducted. With outbound calls, the system furnishes the agent with detailed customer information and a customized, on-screen script, resulting in more personalized, natural conversations. In addition to eliminating nonproductive calls, the system prompts the operator with different questions to ask, based on previous answers. Agents can also view the calling patterns of customers, allowing recommendations of particular long-distance plans.

With inbound calls, the system captures the incoming phone number and uses historical databases to determine where to connect the caller. The call is forwarded to an operator who specializes in a particular type of service or the same operator the customer spoke with on his/her last call.

To ensure the success of future telemarketing campaigns, connections to a central database permit real-time updates to prospects or existing customer records. From a management perspective, the system tracks agent calls and efficiency with colorful charts and graphs. This allows managers to examine trends and make decisions on how to modify the campaign.

center technologies that better integrate information systems, the data that they hold, and typical telephone services. The goal of customer satisfaction and increased sales is at the forefront for these companies. By leveraging information that they already have, they can use call center technology as a strategic weapon.

SALES FORCE AUTOMATION— A GROWING TREND FOR AN INCREASINGLY MOBILE SALES FORCE

The laptop computer has changed the way that sales forces work. By connecting from the road and having the ability to take the computer on sales calls, salespeople can more effectively:

- Enter orders
- Scan and become informed on new products
- Produce product information for existing or prospective customers
- Communicate with others at the company

This makes the worker out in the field as effective as the worker at the office. The reality is that many companies that have appropriately automated their sales and marketing processes have reduced costs, decreased fulfillment time, and increased flexibility in the customization of the product or service.

It is important to embark on a sales force automation project in a structured way. There are three elements that are common when facing an automation process:

- Selection of hardware and software—Of course, a laptop computer is needed. Given that new brands come out seemingly every week with better memory, processor speed, display technology, and battery life, it would be ludicrous to suggest a configuration. However, the unfortunate side effect here is that constant obsolescence will occur. Therefore, be prepared to replace one-third of the inventory every year or so. Other than the connection technology that typically comes with the computer, the more difficult choices will come with the selection of software. The battle will be purchase or develop internally.

Stellar Performer:
Cadence Design Systems

Cadence Design Systems provides electronic design automation services and technology for the world's leading electronic companies. Cadence solutions are designed to accelerate and manage the design of semiconductors, computer systems, networking and telecommunications equipment, consumer electronics, and a variety of other electronic-based products.

To maintain rapid growth and its position of market leadership, Cadence desired to increase the effectiveness of its sales organization to sell competitively differentiated high-value solutions. Cadence has a portfolio of 3,000 products and services that requires a sophisticated salesperson to sell. To get its arms around the product mix and to leverage the overall knowledge of the organization for any given account, Cadence decided to develop a sales force automation solution.

Cadence developed a system to allow the sales force to come together for complex deals. The opportunity management system incorporates a comprehensive customer master database supporting over 500 worldwide users, including 250 mobile users, and conducting business in ten languages. All members of the sales teams have access to the same comprehensive information sources and end-user functionality. For any given deal, it is necessary for the sales force to understand existing sales campaigns, have access to contacts, and be able to get at prices for various components on demand.

Source: www.microsoft.com.

*F*ast
*F*orward to the Real World

Interview with Joe Costello—Red-Hot and Righteous

Richard L. Brandt

Joe Costello is a rising star on the high-tech frontier. He's pioneering a new form of cooperation among companies, moving Cadence Design Systems, Incorporated beyond chip design and into consumer electronics. He rails against greed in Silicon Valley and is proposing a new law and order in which the high-tech industry polices itself.

UPSIDE: **Explain to our readers why electronic design automation [EDA] software is important.** COSTELLO: It's the software that engineers use to design all manner of electronics, from integrated circuits to total boxes [computers]. In the 1970s, the software was created and used inside computer companies. In the '80s, a whole new industry started from nothing. Independent companies built the design software for use by the electronics industry. As the tools got more complicated, you couldn't afford to build everything yourself.

Unless you're a company like Intel. Even Intel, although it was probably the last of the American companies to make this shift. They're one of our largest customers.

Intel used to say that one of its advantages over its competitors was that it had such good design software that it could create these very sophisticated chips. That's what everybody said at one point. Eventually, you have to ask the question, "Are design tools and technology really my core competence?" Well, generally not, but is there some piece of it, some particular software package or algorithm that does give you the advantage? So you begin to narrow it down. In many semiconductor companies, there are still specialized tools and capabilities particular to the company, where they think they have some advantage. A lot of that may be delusional. Our tools run the gamut of IC design, plus application-specific integrated circuits [ASICs] and circuit board designs. That doesn't mean we do every single tool for every single

(Continued)

(Continued)

thing. Our tools span that breadth, and you can do most things with Cadence software. But there are a lot of other companies in this market, and everybody buys a combination of Cadence software and other people's software to get their jobs done.

And your business is changing again. After a period when the company's growth slowed dramatically, you discovered your products were too complicated for your customers to use, so you went into the service business. That's exactly right. In the '90s, we're seeing a transformation into something bigger and of more value to the customers. In the old days, five, 10 years ago, it was straightforward how you put things together. You were dealing with 50,000 transistor chips, as opposed to 5 million. We'd go into these companies and they would tell us our stuff doesn't work. It turned out they weren't using the products correctly.

We realized that the solution was that someone had to step back and look at the bigger picture. Someone had to take responsibility for that business-process reengineering. We should change our business. That's what the customer needs. Let's retool ourselves for that set of skills, and that way we'll be able to deliver this technology to the customer more effectively. And that's what started the process.

When did you start this? The "aha!" experience was in 1991. In 1992, we tried to do some of this ourselves. That's when we became convinced we didn't have the skills either! [Laughs] We had new respect for our customers, too.

So why not just have a separate company specialize in that integration and training? It's a complicated question. There is a new kind of company emerging, and we just happened onto this. You're going to see more of this in the technology space and maybe more in other areas, too. It's taking the raw technology and combining it with services for a solution. It's extremely powerful.

Some people say, "You're going to be jamming your tools down their throats when they want somebody else's." There's some natural skepticism about that. You know what the real story is? Most customers want a solution. They're not so concerned about the underlying engine and technology. We also became more open in our philosophy toward other tools and technology, so in almost every situation, half the technology our people are using to put together these design environments comes from other companies.

(Continued)

(Continued)

Given your tendency toward acquisitions to fill out your product line, it sounds to me like you also have an ideal setup here to figure out whom to acquire. Absolutely true! [Laughs] When you wear your customers' shoes like that, it gives you great insight. Is this technology so key and far ahead that we should acquire it? Or is this technology neat, great and important, but just an adjunct, and what we need to do is form a good relationship with that company so we always have access to that tool?

Oh, come on, the third scenario's got to be that you see they've got a good idea so you just steal it! No, no, no! [Laughs] We don't do stealing!

All right, let's not say steal, but let's say . . . legally clone the process. If we see something good, could we go out and develop something on our own? Yeah, if we have the core competence. But the problem in technology is, it moves so fast. If someone has a product that our service people are using and making successful, the chances of catching up in a window of relevance are slim.

What about the case where you have a competing product, but your design team is using somebody else's product because theirs is better? That's a good place to have a horse race. [Laughs] Then our technology people ought to be motivated to catch up and pass.

So you feel this is a new model for a company? This is a brand-new class of company. It's a hybrid [product plus services], with a new culture, new rules.

How do you tell when this hybrid model is the right one, as opposed to a pure product or pure service company? When there's a tight coupling between the technology and the result, and there's a high degree of complexity, you need to put the services and technology together. Another area is in database technology. Companies like Oracle have done this, but I don't think they've gone far enough. They could do more in tightly integrating the technology and the service piece.

One of the interesting things about doing this kind of interview with us is that you probably will end up getting

(Continued)

(Continued)

phone calls from people who will want you to join their boards. Yeah! [Laughs]

With that in mind, I feel I should ask you: You used to be on Oracle's board, where you could have had influence over Oracle's direction in the service businesses. Why were you fired from the Oracle board? It had to do with our selection of applications packages here at Cadence. There were some differences of opinion between [Oracle CEO] Larry Ellison and me about Oracle and the way it was run and where it was headed at the time—in particular, about the applications products. When I joined the board, one of the things I was excited about was a multibillion-dollar opportunity in applications. But SAP ran way out ahead of them.

So you bought SAP's tools? Yeah. At Cadence, we ended up buying SAP tools. Larry treated it like I was trying to send a message or it was a personal affront, and that I was doing it to be vindictive or to make a point. I was not. It was an independent investigation. And I had to be more than cautious, being the president here and on the board at Oracle. It was a good decision. But my point before that was that Oracle wasn't being aggressive enough in the applications business, and it was a tragedy that all that business was going to SAP. Oracle should have captured the lion's share of that. It had the idea and was way ahead, and it didn't run it [the applications business] well.

Let's continue then with the evolution of your business. Next, we said, "We'll bet people are eventually going to want us to build a whole design environment, and maybe even do the design work." But it happened faster than we expected. A couple of years ago, we announced this deal with Unisys, where they essentially asked us to take over their IC design activity.

And you hired the Unisys engineers. One hundred eighty of them. We have since that time done all Unisys's IC and ASIC design. Then many customers started coming to us saying, "Why should I build my own design factory? Why don't I rent time in your design factory?"

Are these Unisys engineers just working on Unisys products, or are they doing work for other customers? No, we've also hired more people, so we've added to that site, and they're

(Continued)

(Continued)

mainly doing non-Unisys work at this point. We want to build and run the best design factories that allow you to do systems in silicon, or, in turn, take that complex piece of silicon and put it into a board. That's our space.

As part of your payment, you've even taken royalties on the chips you help design or equity in the company you're working for. Why that kind of approach? There's going to be more activity in what we call "virtual vertical integration." Instead of big, vertical, monolithic companies, you can take a vertical market and break it up horizontally [giving each piece of the market to a different partner to handle]. You can see that already. Computer companies hire contract manufacturers to do the printed circuit board. Foundries build the chips, we build and run the chip-design factories, distributors handle the distribution.

I'll give you an example. We just signed a deal with a big consumer company. We're putting together some cable-modem products for them. Without us, they would not have the cable modem. They don't have the design skills and we do, from system-level design down to implementing the silicon pieces. But we don't have any manufacturing, we don't have any distribution channel, we don't have any brand name. Separately, each of us could only sit here and go, "That's a cool market over there, but we can't do anything about it." But put us together and you have a virtual vertical company.

How are you compensated for that work? We don't provide all the value, we don't provide most of the value, but we provide a significant fraction of it. We're experimenting with models, quite frankly. Should we be paid by component, by bonus schemes when they achieve certain levels of success, an equity stake? We're looking for a way to get the right requisite value as we build these virtual vertical companies.

Why is this virtual vertical company trend going to happen now in the computer and semiconductor industries? There's a big trend that is not getting acknowledged: Electronics in the next five years will go through a complete shift to a consumer market. Electronics is almost a trillion-dollar market. There's only one kind of market that can affect a trillion-dollar industry: It's got to be a consumer market. Nothing else is big enough. It's not something that 10 million people want, but something that 100 million people want, or

(Continued)

(Continued)

it isn't going to wiggle the needle in electronics. And everybody wants to wiggle the needle if you want high growth.

So these computer devices move beyond the hands of the elite and are now used by everybody. Yeah. And that's only going to go hog-wild during the next few years. Every interesting opportunity is a consumer opportunity.

A consumer market is very different; it's explosive. That's the good news. But the flip side is that consumers are fickle. They're fashion-oriented, and you have to have a different mind-set. We're not marketing to consumers well. High-technology marketing is atrocious. A lot of the marketing material sounds like plumbers' journals. This is 1997, for Christ's sake; it's a trillion-dollar market! We're not talking up what's hot and interesting in the revolution. And you've got to do that—you've got to preload the consumer. Intel and Microsoft are starting in the right direction—Microsoft is probably the best of the breed. But they're an order of magnitude off of where they need to be to play in the consumer game.

The other side of that is, it puts a different kind of time-to-market pressure on the industry. It will change the whole landscape. Silicon will be a lot more important five years from now for a simple reason: It's the only way you can build an economical system. It's the great consumerizer. We have to start chasing the customer, and the speed's going to be different. Consumer companies are not organized the way we are. This is guerrilla warfare. We have to change our style, our focus, our marketing, and how fast we move.

The winners will be the ones that can get to market the fastest with the exciting product. Look at the Sony PlayStation vs Nintendo 64. If Nintendo 64 had been out at the same time as the Sony PlayStation—when it was originally supposed to be—there wouldn't be a Sony PlayStation.

To get to market faster, companies will be more willing to play in this horizontal approach. Outsourcing things. You do what you're best at, your partners do what they're best at.

Here's another great example. I had a conversation in December with a cable-channel guy who came to one of our executive forums. He was one of the cofounders of MTV, and he did Nickelodeon and ESPN 2. He has a new idea for a cable channel. Actually, someone else had the idea and contacted him and said, "Can you do a cable channel out of this?" He went to see if there was a base of consumers who would pay $10.95 per month for it. He found out there are tens

(Continued)

(Continued)

of millions of people who will if there is a certain set of features. To get those features, he needs to build a widget. So he came to us. We're a godsend to him. He's not going to get the big guys to build it yet, but we'll build it and get the momentum going. Eventually, we hope Motorola and Texas Instruments will be building it.

That's a different kind of market, a different kind of player. We need to create an environment where you can get those creative minds bringing new ideas in. The thing I'm worried about is that we have the potential of throttling our own business. We want every MTV guy on Earth, every one of those creative minds thinking of neat, new consumer ideas, and making it easy for them to implement their ideas. That's how we're going to get from $1 trillion to $2 trillion as an industry. It's by opening up, getting more horizontal, and letting everybody do their piece.

This doesn't displace Intel, Toshiba, and companies like that from designing and building high-volume chips. They'll take over when this product starts shipping in volume. We do the early stage. The prototype, which once was a few units that sat in the lab, will now be something that ships in quantities of a few hundred thousand or a few million.

Source: Richard L. Brandt, "Interview with Joe Costello—Red-Hot and Righteous," Upside magazine (June 1997).

Editor's Note: In October 1997, Costello left Cadence after 13 years at the helm to take a position as vice chairman of Knowledge Universe, a Burlingame, California-based start-up that offers training and educational products and services. Richard Brandt is editor of Upside magazine.

Because this is a growing industry, it is probably best to purchase. However, this can only work if the valuable data embedded in the company's existing systems can be unleashed.

- Train the sales force and gain acceptance—Training is absolutely necessary. Sometimes, even the most basic of computer skills needs to be taught. In addition to the applications that the salespeople will need to be trained on, it is critically important that they understand as much as possible about making connections to the computers back at headquarters. A great deal of the salesperson's time, as well as the support staff's time, can be burned up if this is not done properly.

- Evaluation of business impact—A company should know ahead of time what it expects to gain by deploying sales force automation. Thus, understanding the benefits and costs, either tangible or intangible, must be done.

CHAPTER 7

Emerging Technologies: A Manager's Three-Year Plan

Businesspeople and technology managers alike need to understand the trends in computing. As mentioned many times throughout this book, technology is becoming a larger and larger amount of the overall economy. So, even if your company is satisfied with what it has already, it is not feasible to stop investing in new technologies.

As a businessperson, it is important to separate out the signal from the noise. Many technologies come with lots of hype regarding what they can do for the business. The fanfare and marketing alone sometimes make them successful long before they are proven.

In this chapter, we will examine several of the emerging and important technologies that everyone in a leadership position needs to understand. These technologies are not totally new, and, in fact, the use of many of them was referred to earlier in the book. However, shifts in industry or their potential uses may or will change within the next three to five years, making them important to cover by themselves. The goal of this chapter is to:

- Describe the technologies
- Illustrate their uses and potential impact
- Present case studies
- Help navigate some of the issues and potential pitfalls that may arise

 **THE IMPORTANT EMERGING TECHNOLOGIES**

The Internet

You would have had to be hiding under a rock somewhere not to be cognizant of the explosion of the Internet all around. It was less than four years ago that the first Web browsers were introduced, and the whole Internet mania did not really take off in earnest until 1995. Nevertheless, most of us have been swept up by the hype, and it looks like the Internet is here to stay. As managers, we need to decide how to take advantage of the Net in our business. Should it be leveraged for electronic commerce, should it merely be used as an internal collaboration tool, as a way to work with customers? How much should be invested? Do we need our own Web page? Seems we do. According to a January 1997 Internet Domain Survey, there are currently over 16 million hosts vying for our attention, which translates into literally billions of users—and growing.

Beyond that, there is still tremendous investment going on. Web start-ups are going public all the time, from providers of search engines to backup software. In addition, there seems to be an almost universal concession that the Internet will be a substantial forum for electronic commerce within the next few years.

Java

Just a few years ago, one would only think of a cup of coffee when faced with the word Java. Now, Sun Microsystems, Java's creator, has successfully put the word Java into the mainstream business vernacular.

To most people, Java is a new programming language that is gaining tremendous popularity by the minute. In reality, it is the promise of a new computing paradigm that has endeared computer and businesspeople alike to Java. The use of Java is greatly enabled by the Internet, because the interface for many Java programs is the browser that most of us are now familiar with. The promise being offered that excites everyone is the idea of *write once, run everywhere.* In essence, regardless of the type of computer that is being used, the same computer program can execute on it with the same results for the user. This, of course, saves programming time and eliminates the cross-platform incompatibilities that we all suffer with.

This write-once-run-everywhere concept has nothing to do with Java the programming language, but more to do with something called the "Java Virtual Machine." The Java Virtual Machine finds it way onto almost every computer in one way or another and, thus, enables the write-once-run-everywhere paradigm.

Advances in Networking

Computers have been connected together on networks for decades now. The reason that networking is still an emerging technology is that the rules of the game are changing. The first breakthrough is the cost of capacity, or bandwidth, itself. With domestic deregulation and the same expected internationally, companies can simply buy more capacity, enabling the passing of more information faster and cheaper. On the heels of cheaper access to network capacity is the dire need for it. Large companies are continuing to look for new markets throughout the world to keep profits coming. As companies become global, the need to pass information around the world is critical.

Data Warehousing

Companies are getting bigger and bigger with more and more customers. Over time, a huge amount of information about customers, products, operations, and finance has been accumulated. Many companies are starting to deal with the realities of trying to manage the vast amount of information, whereas others are looking at the information as the crown jewel by which they can gain competitive advantage. The information that a company has in its corporate databases is essentially the knowledge that it has gained over the years.

Data-warehousing technologies allow companies to store the information in one place in a reliable way. In addition, they allow for the information to be available for a large number of users with different needs. Thus, with the information being better managed in some type of centralized place, the company can use it to improve customer contact, identify key customers, as well as purge those that are unprofitable.

Groupware, Workflow, and Collaboration

At the start of the 1990s, businesses were faced with reengineering. Reengineering was a process-based approach to radically improve a company's operations. Although the reengineering fad has generally dissipated, processes are important enough that the father of reengineering has termed the 1990s as the process decade.

Technology has become more and more important to process improvement. In the beginning, technology was used to automate rather mundane tasks that workers typically executed. However, now and in the future, technology will start to enable even the more difficult-to-understand knowledge processes that companies have. Employees have a need to collaborate on projects and generally share information. Although electronic mail assists this to some extent, newer technologies try to put more structure in information storage, retention, and retrieval. At the same time, to eliminate wasteful paperwork or to meet extreme time-to-markets demands, companies need sophisticated workflow systems to move processes along. Not too long ago, these workflow-related projects were expensive automation exercises with a large amount of custom development. Now, companies are looking to the marketplace to find generic but high-powered technologies that can be incorporated in a less costly and a less time-consuming way.

Enterprise Systems Management

There is more and more technology in every company. As technology costs become a greater part of expenses at companies, an emphasis is shifting to the total cost of ownership of the technology investment. To protect from linear or explosive growth in long-term operating expenses relating to technology, many companies are starting to reach for technology that helps manage technology. There are more than a few software companies offering systems that help monitor desktop equipment, computer servers, databases, and networks. The focus of these technologies is to reduce overall costs of technology over time, as well as to provide proactive messages and alerts, so that the technology operators can ensure greater availability.

USE OF INTERNET TECHNOLOGY WITHIN THE COMPANY— INTRANETS

At this point, most people have a common understanding of the Internet. Many companies have started to realize that the same technologies that make the Internet work can benefit them greatly when it comes to internal technology projects. Many companies are creating internal internets, or as the business vernacular calls them, intranets. These intranets are merely a private version of the Internet built, maintained, and used within a single company. Intranets are extremely popular and are becoming more so every day. What are the reasons that intranets are gaining quite a bit of corporate mindshare?

Ubiquitous Technology

Because the Internet has become so popular, almost every computer today comes Internet-ready. In simple terms, this means that they are able to connect to a network and are equipped with a browser, the software that is used to access Internet content.

At the same time, inside the company, many companies have already invested in local- and wide-area network technologies to allow for groups, departments, and offices, both domestically and internationally, to send information to each other in a near real-time manner. Although there are certainly capacity issues, the use of the existing technology infrastructure is quite handy for the creation of an intranet.

Ease of Use

The Web has two fundamental components that make it an easy technology for people to use.

- A single, simple user interface—The browser is *the* way to access the Internet. People have become used to the point-and-click, address-driven way to get at Internet content. If we could only get rid of those ridiculous uniform resource locators (URLs), the world would be much friendlier.

- A simple language for creating information content—Most Web pages are designed using the Hypertext Markup Language (HTML). This is a fairly simple scripting language that the browser knows how to parse to make the Web page appear. In fact, HTML is so simple that many people are able to create their own personal Web page, even though they have no formal training in computer programming. This is only going to get simpler. In fact, new versions of word processors are equipped with automatic storage of documents in Web-enabled format. For the intranet, all of this makes almost everyone capable of making content available to others within the company.

Rapid Information Availability

After data is made available on the intranet, all one needs to know is the address (URL) to get them to it, and away they go. It is really that simple.

Ease of Application Creation and Delivery

We have already discussed the ease of creating Web content. These types of Web applications are not only easy to create, but they are also easy to deliver. By using the browser, there is no longer a need to deploy software on each individual PC or workstation. In the past, application delivery has been a limiting factor for time-to-market, as well as software incompatibility, possibilities that are almost endless.

Although the application delivery advantage is here to stay, the creation of applications will become more difficult as the intranet is used for more sophisticated business applications. As you have probably noticed, most Web pages are relatively simple information displays or repositories. There are some that also use crude interfaces to databases to allow for such things as order entry. The application capability of the Web will increase dramatically as technologies, such as Java, become more widely used. What is Java? More on that later.

CREATION OF CYBERJUNK

Putting up a Web site is pretty easy—almost anyone can do it. The same cannot be said for managing the content for those sites over time. A quick browse around the Internet makes this point. One will find broken links, outdated Web sites, and seemingly abandoned content—in essence, cyberjunk. This same can easily happen on an intranet. Without an idea of how content should be managed, by whom, and how it is going to be kept up to date, the intranet will become a steaming garbage heap of data. Once people cannot find information that they need, or the information is old and out of date, they will lose faith and simply not use it.

THE GREAT PROMISE OF THE INTERNET IS FOR ELECTRONIC COMMERCE

The Internet started out as a government experiment and has turned into a vehicle of interconnectedness for millions of people throughout the world. Despite all of the consumers of the Internet, the financial wealth generated because of it has yet to be realized. Sure, there are quite a few companies that are doing business with customers and suppliers over the Net. In addition, many Web page companies are sponsored by advertisers, similar to looking at cars involved in a NASCAR race.

The true promise for the Internet revolves around its ability to support electronic commerce in a safe, easy, and secure way. Electronic commerce is a now overused term that, to a large degree, confuses people as to its true meaning. Some companies believe that their mere Web presence signifies that they are involved in electronic commerce. Others perform electronic transactions with customers and suppliers on private networks that could certainly be considered electronic commerce—but off-net. This chapter attempts to clear up this confusion.

To explore the definition of electronic commerce, as well as some of its key components, an on-line article by Jack Shaw is adapted below.[1] Before defining the requisite parts of electronic commerce, an example of how it works should shed some light.

A good example of a process that can be supported by electronic commerce is purchasing. The information system built to support this process would be able to issue requests for quotations, process incoming quotes, initiate purchase orders, and so on.

Here's how it would work: An employee might access the system directly, through an intracompany or intranet Web site. However, it is also possible that another application—such as an inventory control system—might detect a reorder point, calculate an order quantity, and pass on a requisition without human intervention.

Regardless of the source, the purchasing application has some work to do. The system must:

- Determine whether the item is established in the system.

- Check whether it has established vendors or whether it needs to identify potential vendors.

- Get availability and pricing.

- Figure out which vendor to place the order with.

- Place the order.

- Pay for the item or confirm credit.

- Verify receipt.

At each of these steps, the purchasing system's rules may call for human intervention, but in the next five to ten years, transactions will become increasingly automated.

If potential vendors must be identified, the system may either launch a Web browser for human use or delegate intelligent software agents to search the Web.

After vendors are identified, the system (or person) places the order. Payment may transpire through credit cards, digital cash transaction, third-party payment services, or confirmation of credit combined with traditional billing and payment. Naturally, authentication and encryption technologies are used.

If the item being purchased is an information product or service, it will be delivered digitally. If it is a physical good or service, confirmation of delivery will be communicated electronically within the organization and to the vendor.

In the near term, many vendors may be contacted by traditional, value-added, network-based electronic data interchange (EDI), electronic mail, or fax. In the longer term, intelligent agents launched by rules-based systems will exchange most of the information over the Internet.

As this happens, EDI and E-mail response times will be reduced to minutes or even seconds. Vendors that cannot respond quickly and accurately will be unable to compete.

Today, many organizations are successfully faking it by getting employees to respond rapidly to EDI and E-mail requests for proposals and purchase orders. But as required response times drop to minutes, then seconds, only rules-based systems will be able to handle transaction volume quickly and accurately enough to meet expectations. Employees will deal with occasional exceptions that the automated systems can't handle, and they will manage the effectiveness and improvement of the overall business process.

Now that we have a working example of electronic commerce, we can describe each of its components.

APPLICATIONS

Typical applications may include purchasing, accounts payable, general ledger, inventory, asset maintenance, cash management, order management, production scheduling, and claims processing. Individuals themselves may initiate transactions, but increasingly, applications will start transactions without human intervention. For example, an inventory control system may detect a reorder point, calculate an order quantity, and pass a requisition to the purchasing system.

The applications send messages to the electronic commerce broker. Each message identifies the sender and recipient, the message type (purchase order, receipt), and the message contents.

Electronic Commerce Broker

The electronic commerce broker takes messages from the application and then translates, addresses, formats, and routes them to the appropriate communications interface. Brokers use directory services built into the system to look up addresses and route messages to a fax number or Internet, value-added network, or E-mail address.

For traditional EDI, the electronic commerce broker would also create the appropriate EDI format. Acknowledgments and other responses are passed back to the electronic commerce broker for logging or forwarding back to the appropriate application. Other broker functions include archiving, reporting, and auditing messages.

Communications Interface

This software module formats and transmits the message over one (or more) communications medium, be it an EDI mailbox, a fax, an Internet mailbox, or an intelligent agent. It was designed as a separate software component to allow for additional electronic commerce media in the future. Whereas the electronic commerce broker handles the authenticated information in plain text, the communications interface is responsible for all of the necessary security-related conversions.

An intelligent agent is a rules-based application that can transport itself from site to site over the Internet in search of requested information.

Corporate Firewall

The corporate firewall protects data, messages, and other resources from the outside world. Some technologies, such as the EDI mailbox and the corporate Web server, exist both inside and outside the firewall.

External Network

Trading partners are accessible via telephone, public VAN, or the Internet. Any trading partner can be accessed through any of the three types of networks.

Trading Partner

Trading partners are all those external organizations with which a company exchanges information. Each may have a Web site and/or a communications gateway. They could include the following:

- Vendor
- Customer
- Bank

- Transportation carriers
- Insurance companies
- Government
- Healthcare providers
- Trade exchange
- Electronic catalogs
- Credit card authorization

INFORMATION SECURITY IS AN IMPORTANT PART OF ANY INTERNET STRATEGY

Doing business on the Internet is becoming a way of life, but a lack of security can quickly wipe things out or, at a minimum, greatly shake consumer confidence. There are three aspects to security that a company needs to consider when developing an Internet strategy.

First, the company needs to fortress itself off from intruders. This is typically done through something called firewalls. A firewall is a technology that blocks intruders from getting at internal company information via outside connections to the Internet. It essentially enables outsiders to do only what you want them to do and prevents them from doing anything else.

Second, within the company, it is not always appropriate for everyone to see everything. So, just like with most systems, it is imperative that authorization and authentication take place for users trying to gain access to resources. This is easy to say but difficult to manage. With the ease that nonprogrammer types can develop applications that access databases, computer security personnel must be on the lookout for unapproved access to data in the firm.

Third, to enable any type of electronic commerce, privacy for transactions is essential. A great deal of innovation in the way of public key encryption and digital signatures is going on. These technologies show promise in ensuring that transactions are safe in terms of people or companies being verified as to identity, as well as the encryption of the actual transactions.

To make these elements part of a strategy, companies must ensure that they employ expertise in computer security. Without knowledge of what

Stellar Performers: Electronic Commerce Trailblazers—On-Line Stock Sale Companies

From January to March 1997, according to Piper Jaffray Research, there was an average of 95,500 Web-based stock transactions executed per day. Companies such as Charles Schwab, E*Trade, and Fidelity Investments lead the way as providers of on-line trading services. This market is growing, proving that electronic commerce on the Net is a reality. In fact, Forrester Research predicts that there will be 3 million on-line investor accounts by the end of 1997, and that number will surge to upward of 14 million by the year 2002. By providing software and near real-time market quotes to consumers connected to the Internet, companies allow for the consumer to trade without talking to a broker. This fuels the fire for increased intraday trading activity by individual investors. Why all the excitement? Of course, electronic trading costs less than calling the brokerage directly and having them execute the trade for you.

In addition, the electronic brokerage providers have been able to prevent security breaches by ensuring their internal sites are fire-walled and providing encryption on transactions.

The next plunge for these companies will be to increase capacity to allow for heavier and heavier trading volumes without significant performance delays for the investors. At the same time, the industry needs to capture more investors that are not scared of doing business on the Net or with a computer.

hackers can do and how to protect systems, a company is operating at an extreme risk.

MOVING FROM INTRANETS TO EXTRANETS

According to *Information Week,* nearly one in five companies with Web sites have opened up their corporate intranet to customers and suppliers. This is intercompany communication in the information age. More formally, research firm ActivMedia's random study of 3,500 commercial Web sites defined extranets as Internet Protocol (IP) networks used for maintaining ongoing business relationships while enabling private, security, and customized communication.[2]

LIMITATIONS THAT COULD LIMIT THE LONG-TERM USEFULNESS OF THE INTERNET

While many people believe that the Internet is, or is close to, becoming the future for company-to-company transactions and consumer commerce, there are a whole range of issues that may limit its growth or acceptance as a significant market factor. Several of these issues are explored below.

Capacity Limits

There is a constant concern about capacity. As more and more users and companies use the Net for information gathering as well as commerce, there is constantly a need for more network capacity between locations and within the servers and other equipment that pass information from one place to another.

The Internet Is Currently a Nondeterministic Technology

The design of the Internet precludes (at the current time) predictable and assured connection speeds from location to location. Conceptually, think of the Internet as a cloud. Your business location and its connection to the cloud are fairly well understood. However, after the data enters the cloud, it is nondeterministic as to what may happen. There could be a few hops to the final destination or a multitude. Overall, this leads to spotty, ill-determined

Stellar Performer:
Xilinx, Incorporated

Xilinx, Incorporated, a $571 million semiconductor manufacturer in San Jose, California, uses an extranet to communicate with manufacturers in Asia and sales contractors throughout the world. The need for a reliable extranet stems from the fact that Xilinx has 300 sales representatives throughout the world that actually work for a myriad of contracting agencies.

In the past, Xilinx used the usual forms of communication in dealing with these salespeople—fax and mail. There was a constant need for information and a flood of paper. Now, the sales representatives are able to access internal Xilinx systems via the worldwide Web. This enables the sales representatives to accurate, timely information delivered much more cheaply and quickly than before. Xilinx uses commercially available software to provide authentication for these sales representatives.

Similarly, Xilinx has opened up its systems via the Web for Asian manufacturers. Just by sending an E-mail, notifying the manufacturers that a design change has been made or completed, the manufacturers can enter the system to get the latest information without waiting for sometimes slow carriers.

Xilinx has captured several of the key values of intercompany communication via the Internet—timely and accurate information. They are also interested in processing financial transactions after they feel the security is adequate and that they have a workable solution.

Source: Information Week *(9 June 1997).*

performance characteristics. For recreational use, many people can get over this. However, for critical, time-sensitive business applications, this is a serious problem. The challenge in the future will be the development of technologies that allow the Internet to become not only stable, but a place where performance can be that of a private network.

Security Concerns

Ever since the Internet became popular, the largest knock that it has is that it is considered to be nonsecure. In essence, because there are security issues, the Internet could never be used as a wide-scale place for commerce to occur. There are concerns that credit card information will be stolen; company systems can be easily infiltrated, allowing for access to trade secrets; and that once information about people gets into cyberspace, privacy will go out the window.

Understanding that this issue is in the minds of most people, IBM has responded in the media in a very broad way. In a recent advertisement campaign, IBM has put Internet security into the forefront. They are saying that they understand it is important and are doing something about it.

Standards

A lack of standards in the industry among the vendors trying to get a slice of the pie could be the death knell for Internet. Successful, ubiquitous technologies, such as the telephone system (some may claim this was due to a monopoly) and broadcast television, were successful, because the people trying to make money from the industry were interested in creating and enforcing standards. In the Internet world, each vendor is trying to do something to differentiate themselves. This sometimes leads to problems in compatibility. For instance, even at the browser level, one of the fundamental building blocks, we see Web sites that do not work properly across the two major browser vendors, Microsoft and Netscape.

Consumer Comfort

People embrace change very slowly. The creation of direct catalog sales did not kill the malls. There should not be an expectation that the Internet will kill either direct catalog sales or the malls. We should expect the evolution to take place slowly. The general population needs to get more comfortable with computers, security needs to be solved, and the experimental nature of many Internet sites needs to be modified before complete adoption as an electronic commerce or entertainment vehicle. Although these issues will more than likely be resolved, there is a chance that a bubble has been created in terms of expectations. Thus, the promise will not take place quickly, and the investment will dry up before it does.

 ## COMPANIES NEED TO HAVE POLICIES ON INTERNET USAGE

As more and more companies get connected to the Net, a whole new wave of issues relating to employee management and legalities arises. The two main problems facing companies are employee productivity and corporate liability. Thus, it is important to have corporate policies on Net usage. All employees need to understand:

- The purpose of the policy
- Guidelines for acceptable and unacceptable Internet use
- Guidelines for software/downloading
- Copyright issues
- Computer security
- Consequences for policy violations

In terms of productivity, in the old days, if an employee was using a computer, he or she was probably working. Now at one's fingertips are computer games, travel networks, shopping malls, up-to-the-minute sports statistics, and schedules. This can be an extreme waste of company resources in terms of people's time. In addition, Internet traffic can clog corporate networks.

On the legal front, the countless sites specializing in illicit material, including sexually explicit pictures, weapons procurement, and illegal information, pose a threat to every company. Downloads of this information or resending it from within the corporation may expose the company to potential liability.

The good news is that in addition to corporate policies, companies can use technology to manage this new technology. New technologies have been developed specifically to monitor Internet access. These programs provide reports on what sites are accessed by whom, when they are accessed, plus how much data was downloaded. In addition, there are programs to block specified Internet sites, removing temptation and preventing inappropriate access by employees.

In a proactive manner, these technologies allow companies to see how the Internet is being used. This allows the company to make modifications to policies and technologies over time to enhance productivity.

A term that many business managers have been hearing about in recent years is *data warehousing*. Data warehousing is a computer term for the consolidated storage of a company's information. This information can span a wide range of possibilities. For instance, a firm can really gain insight into what its most important customers are by examining information consolidated in one place. A manager could query the database to find out which customers have spent the most over time, how long it took to make a sale to the customer, and even the internal cost of maintaining the account in sales and support time and effort. Data warehousing to the business manager should be synonymous with looking at information in a structured approach.

THINGS TO LOOK OUT FOR AND GOOD PRACTICES WHEN BUILDING A DATA WAREHOUSE

A warehouse is typically a database of historical and functional business information. The novel idea, though, is that it is arranged according to business logic rather than computer logic, allowing users to query it at will for whatever information is relevant to making business decisions.

For all of its promises, building a data warehouse can be even more challenging than planning a space shuttle launch. This is one of those technology initiatives that cannot succeed without extensive user involvement. A good warning comes from the past two conferences of the Life Office Management Association (LOMA), a member organization for companies in the life insurance industry. Its conferences draw attendees with job titles ranging from the systems manager level up to senior managers. In 1995, 91 percent of about 50

LOMA conference attendees said their warehouses had failed to generate a return on investment. In 1996, 85 percent of a comparable number of respondents had the same response. Interestingly, none of those surveyed attributed the failures to technical problems. The problem, they said, was that the projects didn't answer a business need. In other words, users weren't consulted during the design phase of the warehouse projects.[3]

There are several ways to engage users and to make warehouses a wonderful success.

- Information technology organizations that understand the industry well—When IT groups know the industry, the chances for success are much higher. Clearly, the forces behind a tele-communications data warehouse are likely to be radically different from that of a health care warehouse. By analyzing major industry forces and ensuring that the team building the warehouse are not merely technicians, the IT organization is posed to add tremendous value to the effort.

- Ensuring that the warehouse meets the needs of the users—More than any other IS project, a warehouse must conform to users' needs. Instead of participating in the projects, users almost have to lead the development effort to ensure that the warehouse contains the right data in the right format.

- Choosing the correct sizing for the project—There is always the risk of not choosing the appropriate scope for the project. Warehouses can be implemented in a massive effort spanning the entire enterprise or in a more manageable departmental approach. The two factors that must be set straight are the expectations of the businesspeople as to what they can get out of the investment and the overall budget. As long as all parties involved jointly reach the decisions on these two issues, scope decisions should be less of a problem.

DATA WAREHOUSES CAN IMPROVE THE CORPORATE BOTTOM LINE

A great number of technology investments are very difficult to quantify in terms of financial impact. Perhaps that is one of the reasons that companies are embracing data-warehousing technologies and that the businesspeople tend to understand its value.

Through the use of data warehousing, companies can directly attribute the success of marketing campaigns and specific customer retention strategies. More importantly, it is through this technology that companies can actually form the strategies to begin with. When designed properly, warehouses can produce astounding business paybacks. According to a recent IDC Canada survey, the average ROI for implementing a data warehouse over a three-year period was 401 percent.[4]

Take the case of Union Pacific Railroad. They were aiming to provide a warehouse that could be used across the firm 24 hours a day, seven days a week. The overall goal was to improve the organization's bottom line. With a data warehouse managing more than 600 gigabytes of data from multiple subject areas, Union Pacific secured a $14 million annual ROI. In addition, a welcome side effect due to the effort was a discovery of needless overpayment in state taxes of $1 million per year. Other benefits directly attributed to the effort included large savings due to shipping goods only when the delivery charges were paid and better use of their own rail cars, allowing for significant savings.[5]

 Data warehousing depends on good data. If the information in current databases is inaccurate or incomplete, it is likely that the information once combined in a warehouse will suffer the same problems. Thus, extensive costs can come into play if a data-cleansing project is required. In addition, the bottom line is that you end up not getting what was originally expected.

WHY JAVA IS PROMISING

Sun Microsystems and its CEO, Scott McNealy, are pushing the Java programming language as the next generation of computing and as the alternative to the computing model that is put forth by Microsoft. As mentioned earlier in the chapter, the elegance of Java is the concept of *write once, run everywhere*. What McNealy and

Stellar Performer: French National Railroad

Although most American images of railroads are slow freight cars chugging across the country, nothing can be further from the truth in France. With trains that carry passengers at hundreds of miles per hour, the railroad is increasingly a technology innovator and dependent on technology in its services. At the same time, the French National Railroad takes the same approach to its use of IT.

The railroad uses a sophisticated system encompassing distribution, reservations, passenger yield management, fleet optimization, marketing, and accounting. The important point is that the applications draw on a single data warehouse for its information. Thus, with confidence, the applications can make automatic decisions on factors such as fare availability. Those decisions are input directly into the railroad's operational systems.

Because the railroad greatly depends on revenues from its high-speed trains, optimization of equipment availability is vital to forecasting traffic loads and prices. Before implementing a data-warehousing strategy, this optimization was done, but not efficiently. This left an exposure where airlines could tap into market share by discounting fares at particular times.

The data warehouse helps the railroad in the following ways:

- Marketing, commercial, and accounting functions—The warehouse contains a rich mix of information on travelers, fares, and other available services. For example, marketing analysts can see where travelers on particular routes purchased tickets, how much they paid, and whether they requested meals during the trip or rental cars at their destinations.

- Yield management—The operational goal of the railroad is to maximize the use of each train up to five minutes before it leaves the station. Thus, the yield management system needs to draw on historical and real-time information collected from the warehouse to forecast demand and maximize capacity. The system anticipates how many people will request seats on a particular train and day, in a particular market, at a particular price, and then makes projections about the number of potential no-shows and overbooks seats accordingly. The system also adjusts the number of discount fares on each train, based on demand, maximizing passenger revenues, and improving customer service by making appropriately priced seats available. Those decisions automatically are input back into the reservation system in real-time.

Source: Adapted from the Data-Warehousing Institute's Web site.

Sun are really trying to dig into is the issue of total cost of ownership.

For the last five years or so, industry groups have been publishing statistics regarding total cost of ownership of a PC. At the high end, there are theories that the PC costs a business between eight and ten thousand dollars per year. Of course, only a fraction of this is the hardware and software that is on the machine itself. It is all the buried costs such as networks, updates, support, and end-user trial and error that are the real insidious problems. The cause for this, according to McNealy and the gang at Sun, is the fat client computing model that Microsoft has pushed society and businesses into. This fat client model requires more computing power, more disk, more complexity, and, therefore, more maintenance over time.

So, here comes Java, the idea in its simplest form is that Java can run on every machine, and the execution of the programs can be done over a network. Thus, a bunch of issues are solved, and costs will go down dramatically. The story goes like this. Java allows for a thin client. Programs are not resident on the PC and only get to the device that the end user has at the time they are run. This eliminates the need for all this horsepower on the PC and the perils of distributing new software, as well as all those people that have to come fix the machine when something happens to it.

In this model, businesses will not need expensive desktop machines, the expensive software that runs on them, or the support infrastructure to deal with the machines.

 THE EMERGING JAVA RECRUITING NIGHTMARE

Regardless of whether Java is a long-term commercial success, gives business great gains, or is considered strategic, it will affect all IT organizations. The place that is most likely to be hit first is in the recruiting arena. With the dearth of IT talent out in the market and the accelerating needs, getting young, ambitious computer graduates is the only way to keep costs down and productivity up. Although many companies have jumped on the college-recruiting bandwagon,

Stellar Performer:
Harris Semiconductor

Although more than 90 percent of large organizations have implemented data warehouses, few of those data warehouses have had a more important impact on the success of their organizations than the one at Harris Semiconductor.

The semiconductors that put the intelligence in antilocking brakes, in satellites, in cellular phones, and in hundreds of other products are manufactured by Harris Semiconductor in five plants around the world, from Kuala Lumpur to Melbourne, Florida.

All Harris Semiconductor products pass through multiple manufacturing plants to receive processing specific to each site, and engineers everywhere need data about what happens at every site for yield improvement and performance evaluation. The financial and planning community also needs the data for costing and production management.

To link the engineering facilities worldwide, Harris implemented a data warehouse that logically presents one data source for all users. Thus, Harris users around the company and around the world have transparent access to all the data, regardless of where it originated.

In addition, to reduce wasted effort and to make it easy for Harris's distributed engineering community to work together, Harris created common screens for displaying data in every plant. Before the warehouse was implemented, people in every plant spent time creating data retrieval programs—and all of them were different. The warehouse project radically reduced that redundant effort and, in using common metrics and screen formats, created a whole new level of communication among Harris engineers throughout the world. The system also implements best practices across the company, enabling all locations to use the same metrics and allowing all employees to view the performance statistics for any location, confident the same methodology is being used.

Because every engineer is looking at data that were calculated the same way and displayed in the same format, long-distance telephone communication among them is made easier. They each know where on the screen they must look, and they can talk as if they are standing next to each other looking at the same screen. The system has eliminated disputes over what should be measured or why one facility's measurement system is superior to the others.

Providing information for engineers and planners, on demand, is an important job for the data warehouse, but it is not the most important one. That honor goes to the alarm server and the auto-

(Continued)

(Continued)

mated data-mining facility that Harris implemented to solve a challenging manufacturing problem. The problem occurred when tiny changes in the manufacturing process accumulated to cause semiconductor wafer specifications to change from what was expected and needed. Several years ago, this type of problem accumulated and caused substantial losses in productivity.

So Harris decided to use its warehouse to fix the problem. Harris feeds wafer data from around the world into an analytical database where it is analyzed, using advanced data-mining technology, to find even tiny deviations. When substantial deviations are found, the system itself issues an alert—sending messages to all key people around the world, letting them know that a potential problem has arisen. Before Harris's system was installed, at least one-half dozen failed lots would have been required to gain the engineer's attention and priority. Then the engineer would have run a statistical analysis of the corresponding data. With the new system, a single lot can reveal that a problem exists, with the statistical analysis already performed, and results waiting for the engineers to review.

Source: Data-Warehousing Institute, www.dw-institute.com.

they may have to change their strategy just to bring in top graduates.

The computer industry is already on the verge of the top college candidates saying, "Do you use Java?" or "I would love to come work for you, but I want to program with Java." Answering no to these questions is sure to be a way to lose the candidates that are most desired. Unfortunately, due to this fact, many companies will be forced to adopt Java as a computing paradigm, regardless of whether it will actually benefit them at all. This, in turn, will force companies to retrain the existing technology staff so that they too can program in Java. The short-term effect is retraining, but the long-term effects are more profound. Shifts in computer-programming languages are very expensive. All the existing systems will be written in languages other than Java. Therefore, the IT group will need to employ people that maintain those systems or face rewriting them.

Stellar Performer: CSX

CSX is a multibillion-dollar transportation company. Within 90 days after a CEO edict, CSX deployed a new system for use by seven trial customers. Later, functionality was enhanced over three delivery phases, so that now many more CSX customers can order railroad freight cars, enter and query comprehensive waybill information, track shipments via an interactive map with drill-down capabilities, access account information, and send and receive E-mail.

Application workstations are being deployed in accounting to access billing and account information, on loading docks so that receivers know the contents of containers before they arrive, and in a variety of roles not originally envisioned by CSX or its customers. Indeed, one firm that reships freight through CSX has negotiated a deal to private-label the application and deploy it to their customers. Overall, because the Java-based system does not require software to be distributed on every machine, CSX is gaining more and more unintended but happy users.

Business functionality notwithstanding, the use of the Java at CSX is returning a variety of cost savings. The prior system was not only far less functional than the Java-based one, but it also cost $5 million annually to support. The Java-based replacement was developed and deployed to the first 24 customer firms for less than $1 million. In addition, the Java-based strategy that CSX has adopted will delay the procurement of PCs, because all that is required to run them is a browser.

Moreover, in terms of competitive positioning, CSX's two largest customers—one in autos and the other a shipper of bulk coal—will save $10 million in 1997 as a direct result of efficiencies, lower costs, less expensive client systems, and cheaper communication links made possible by the Java-based system.

Source: JavaWorld.

Stellar Performer: Reuters

Over its 144-year history, Reuters has built its worldwide reputation on giving its customers instant news and information. As a market leader, its main financial products are used in trading floors throughout the world. By embracing the Java-programming language, it now gives customers tools more rapidly to extract additional value from Reuters products and services. Reuters' goal is to reduce time to market, both in developing new products and getting them to the end users.

The current operating model for product delivery at Reuters is for engineers to visit the 35,000 client sites and update the 340,000 Reuters terminals with new software. This model is becoming antiquated because of Java. Because Reuters has one of the largest private global data networks that broadcasts real-time prices, they can use standard Internet protocols over their networks to deliver new products directly to client desktops at almost zero cost.

In addition to rapid product delivery, Reuters has also seen productivity increases through reusing Java software components. Because Java is new, it encourages open communication. Also, using Web technology itself encourages reuse, because it improves communication between developers in cities around the world.

Not to be overlooked are the international capabilities that Java has native to it. Reuters market is global, and users want services and products in their own national languages. Reuters cannot compete without it in Eastern Europe and Asia. This applies to the text on the user interface as well as the content. In the past, the cost of internationalizing products has been high, but Java helps produce localized products and services much more cheaply.

Source: Sun Microsystems. Sun's U.K. Web site.

This can turn into an arms race scenario. The competition will be to get the best people and the greatest number of them. This, in turn, will drive up wages. The bad side effect is that it drives up the wages for the people that support the systems that are considered legacy, because they are not so easy to get rid of, but they are mission critical.

WORKFLOW AND DOCUMENT MANAGEMENT

WHAT ARE THE BENEFITS OF USING DOCUMENT MANAGEMENT?

It is well known that documents represent the know-how of industrial corporations much more than formatted data, but to a large extent, document processing is still based on paper. In addition, it is especially disadvantageous that information that is embedded in paper documents is partly or entirely lost after their active processing has terminated. Then the documents are usually stored in insufficient paper archives or transferred only partly to persistent on-line databases.

Although there has been a shift away from typewriters and secretaries, the panacea of the paperless office will never occur. In fact, because word processors and presentation software are so easy to use, there are more documents than ever being created. To accommodate the explosive growth of documents in most businesses, document management systems allow for the file cabinet of the 1990s to exist—a singular, organized place where the information can be stored and retrieved. This is the simple part.

Thus, as more and more documents are created and as they tie into the company's business processes, it is critical to allow people to share documents sometimes across oceans, as well as to protect documents from eyes that should not see them. So what does a document management system allow an organization to do?

- Simplify computer use in the organization— Because the management of documents can be tied to business processes, the computer becomes a tool that is much easier to use in the context of the work that each employee needs to do.

- Secure documents—Sensitive documents within the system can be secured. In addition, permissions as to who can see what can be controlled at whatever level of the organization makes sense (i.e., workgroup, department, enterprise).

- Control documents—The life of a document can be queried. All document activities can be profiled, tracked, and logged.

- Track versions—Multiple document revisions can be tracked and stored.

- Locate documents—Documents can be searched and retrieved logically and quickly.

- Archive documents—Automate document archiving and deletion.

- Organize documents—Customize and track related group project files.

- Track costs—For those penny-pinching businesses, it is possible to track time, keystrokes, and pages printed for cost control.

WORKFLOW SYSTEMS HELP STREAMLINE BUSINESS PROCESSES

Systems that help to improve workflow are designed to reduce cycle time, to improve the accuracy of the process, and to provide metrics of process performance. Thus, it is necessary to integrate various types of electronic documents and formatted data—different existing and innovative application systems—into a common system to support an overall process. Furthermore, it is necessary to flexibly integrate the business process–related activities into a homogeneous workflow while considering the organizational structure.

Workflow systems aim to model and analyze business processes. The basic idea is this: Information objects (e.g., order application forms) are passed through all stages of a certain business process and are enriched gradually, just like a physical product during the manufacturing process. Thus, the system selects for each activity of the process a proper person who executes the activity and supports the processing by linking suitable application systems. The final product of a workflow, again, is an information object (e.g., the completed order application form).

When setting out to design and implement a workflow system, there are three key things to keep in mind.

- Integrate existing application systems into workflow implementation.
- Develop efficient techniques and methods to support the analysis and modeling of the workflow.
- Design the system with the appropriate controlling tools to enrich the planning and control system processes of a corporation.

The requirements for the system can only be completed when the business process is understood. It is the understanding of the process and the subsequent embedding of the logic into the computer system that is often difficult. To gather the requirements for the system, the following design points are needed.

- Analysis and modeling—The actual processes of the considered environment have to be registered. After an analysis of their weaknesses, the nominal concept is to build either a documented or computer version of the process model as it is understood.
- Definition and configuration—The process model has to be transformed into a workflow model that can be incorporated into a system. The workflow model defines a network of process activities and is the basis for routing and integration. Other views of the process model (e.g., organizational structure, application systems to integrate) have to be understood as well.
- Routing and integration—Based on the workflow model, the system will need to execute the actual process. It usually means routing some piece of work (e.g., work order, engineering drawing) through the entire process.
- Controlling—Controlling functions of the system need to be defined. For example, a failure of a particular task must be rescheduled. In addition, the statistics for process performance must be kept and reported.
- Archiving—After the workflow has been processed, the final product needs to be classified and archived.

WHEN TO CONSIDER USING A WORKFLOW SYSTEM

Clearly, workflow systems do not fit in everything a company does. In its simplest terms, consider workflow systems wherever the business process is structured. For instance, workflow systems do a decent job of helping streamline processes such as order fulfillment. However, they are typically inappropriate for less-structured tasks such as software development. So, simply because there are a series of tasks or processes that help some work get completed, workflow does not always apply.

- Managing dissimilar information formats—Often, workflow systems need to speed along documents that are in different formats. For example, in an order process, there may be facsimiles sent in by customers, scanned paper orders, and internal information sources that require routing. A workflow system uses the tasks that integrate these dissimilar information formats so that all the data required stays in one place and is managed appropriately.

- Process-oriented integration—Workflow systems are useful as tools for process-oriented integration. Single activities or tasks can be flexibly assembled to a process within a workflow system. If the workflow changes, the application systems that are especially designed to support a certain business function do not have to be changed. The process steps can be reorganized as long as the information is available to complete the task.

- Integration of the organizational structure—workflow systems are designed to marry people, process, and technology. This occurs regardless of organizational structure, and, in fact, helps tie together structures. The goal must be to have the most flexible choice of proper users according to the recent workflow status and additional criteria. One concept is the choice of persons according to their organizational roles or job responsibilities. Beyond that, there are more complex selection mechanisms. For example, users may have particular profiles.

- Integration of existing application systems—Another challenge for a workflow system is to

Stellar Performer: Harris Corporation Farinon Division

Harris Corporation Farinon Division is a designer and manufacturer of a broad range of analog and digital microwave radios, lightwave systems, and multiplex communication equipment, with sales in more than 100 countries. Harris Farinon operates three facilities in North America—Redwood Shores, San Antonio, and Montreal. Harris Farinon's customer base includes telephone companies, cellular companies, utilities, pipelines, railways, airports, and all levels of government.

One of the major concerns at Harris was the need to decrease the cycle time on all major business process cycles.

With rapidly increasing demand for Harris products and services, management faced two choices: either to add many more people to meet the demands of the customers or to increase the automation of the existing workforce.

The management decided to pursue a strategic path of using workflow and document management technology to improve the processes of the business. The goal was to eliminate the amount of paper produced and to reduce the cycle time of business processes.

The first process that Harris decided to attack was sales order booking. This is the front-line process that generally impacts the customers first and most directly. By automating the process using workflow software, Harris is now better able to respond to customer demands. In addition, because the routing of sales orders is now done automatically, there is an elimination of paper in the process, making status easier to find and accuracy a great deal better.

Another benefit that Harris gets using its workflow system is flexibility. The market changes constantly, and Harris needs to adapt its processes accordingly. In the old days, when companies merely automated processes, it would have been difficult if not impossible to modify the systems to meet the required process changes. Now, workflow software has inherent flexibility. Process steps can be added, removed, or modified without substantial reprogramming.

enable convenient access to existing application systems that are involved in a process, in the sense of an *intelligent front-end.* Because the results of an application system can be added to the process folder, it is possible to integrate formerly isolated application systems or programs that run on different platforms.[6]

CASE STUDY
Workflow and Information Management Streamline Document Control and Meet FDA Regulations

Equipment depended on for use in life-or-death situations must adhere to the strictest guidelines of the Food and Drug Administration's Good Manufacturing Practices. These practices, directed at manufacturing processes, are designed to help assure the quality and reliability of products. Every step in a product's life cycle, from design through postmarket servicing, must be documented in a compliant manner. Documentation on every field incident, significant design changes, or improvements must be filed with the FDA. A defibrillator manufacturer needed to track this huge volume of information effectively. Using workflow and document management technology, the manufacturer developed an automated product data management and tracking system.

The first phase of the new system required registering index data for the 50,000 pages of records pertaining to the device, which had been released to the FDA, and 250,000 records comprising engineering changes into the database. Under FDA regulations, the records submitted must contain all designs, specifications, manufacturing procedures, quality assurance, and labeling information. At the same time, history records must also be maintained. Specific historical information from all tasks and operations is recorded on specific templates. A variety of reports is generated throughout the manufacturing and filing process. Many of them must be submitted to the FDA for review.

The system deployed performs electronic tracking of the records and gives instant access to the latest version of a document, while also showing the change activity that is outstanding against the document, as well as what the change history has been. Subordinate information, such as detail designs, cost, justification, and validation information, is related through attribute values that can be updated.

An example of the workflow aspects of the system is the processing of engineering change summaries. When an engineering change summary is developed and registered in the database, the workflow system automatically routes it to appropriate individuals in engineering, regulatory affairs, manufacturing, and quality. Their analyses are routed, in turn, to the change board. The responses are not merely static. The system determines the appropriate next steps to take when particular conditions are met.

If the engineering change is rejected, the system automatically sends it to its author for revision and resubmission. If it is finally approved, an implementation plan is added, and the system moves the package to the designer who will make the change. Once the change is implemented, the new document is registered as part of the official record for the product and automatically supersedes previous versions.

Because record keeping accounts for up to 20 percent of violations cited in FDA warning letters, it is imperative that manufacturers take this process seriously. In this case, not only does the new system help the manufacturer with all required regulations, but the automation of the engineering change process, document tracking, and control procedures helps to increase productivity, lower product costs, and assure the highest quality product.

NETWORKS

Data networks are poised to revolutionize the way companies do business. The largest data network available is the Internet. As the Internet gets more popular, it is likely that the capacity will continue to be increased. However, most companies need private or privately managed network to guarantee service for intracompany purposes. Global industries that are part of a series of linked activities compete against rivals on a worldwide basis, trying to achieve economies of scope and scale. Services account for the largest share of gross domestic product in all but the lowest-income

Stellar Performer: Dell Computer

Dell Computer is a high-flying Wall Street darling. Dell Computer has gained a market leadership position as a growing PC manufacturer. The company has achieved this extraordinary growth by pioneering an innovative approach to selling PCs that addresses the problems and inefficiencies of traditional computer dealers.

By enabling customers to buy customized PCs directly from the manufacturer, Dell provides a single source for complete computing solutions. From order to customized manufacture through delivery, technical support, and system disposal, Dell offers direct customer contact and total accountability.

Dell Computer, due to the direct nature of the business, deals with many thousands of accounts in any one month. Their financial control systems provided reports from the Accounts Receivable ledger for collection purposes. However, as the number of transactions grew, it became more and more difficult to handle the outstanding receivables efficiently. It was a time-consuming and efficient task to check on a customer's credit position through the many statements at any point in time and keep an up-to-date view of the collections to be made.

Dell staff, based at the Bracknell European Headquarters, began looking at a number of solutions to the credit problem in the early 1990s. The goal was to support the credit management processes within Dell by linking their existing Accounts Receivable ledger and internal order management system.

Dell turned to a workflow systems solution to help with this process. A key component of the system is the collections module. The new process, enabled by the workflow system, works in the following way.

After analyzing output received from the accounting packages, outstanding invoices are grouped (e.g., by operator, by date, by value) in priority sequence. They are then automatically compiled into an on-line daily worklist for each operator to work on. Thus, the major chore of assigning work is completed by the system, instead of manually. The system bears the brunt of analyzing, updating, and prioritizing the aged debt list. Next, as the workers complete their tasks throughout the day, the results are stored in the system. Thus, at a few clicks on the keyboard, Dell has all the events completed by the worker and the outcome. This can be used to analyze internal processes or in legal processes when required.

Via the workflow system, Dell has reduced its outstanding receivables and is narrowing down the amount of bad debt.

Source: Computer Systems for Business, Ltd.

Stellar Performer:
SunHealth Alliance

One of the nation's largest and oldest alliances of not-for-profit hospitals, SunHealth has partners in 15 states stretching from Maryland to Texas. These partners operate or are affiliated with 300 health care organizations. Together, they comprise approximately 72,000 inpatient beds and provide health services worth more than $24 billion annually.

The difficulty of tracking and accessing thousands of documents was affecting customer service for SunHealth. To ease the strain, SunHealth implemented a document management system that is helping it to respond quickly and efficiently to its partners in the alliance.

SunHealth deals with hundreds of documents each day, including correspondence with partners, internal reports, and research papers. Like many companies, SunHealth had accumulated an enormous amount of documents, but they were unmanaged and even more difficult to share. As a result, SunHealth employees spent an inordinate amount of time tracking down—and sometimes needlessly retyping—documents.

With SunHealth's old system, documents typically could be found only by the creator. If the employee who created a document left the company or simply wasn't in the office, it was next to impossible to locate the document. In contrast, the new system allows anyone with access to the system to find any document in 30 seconds or less. Productivity has increased, because users can now find, revise, and produce documents more efficiently than ever.

Through improved document handling, SunHealth became more efficient in responding to its partners. The document management solution also offers version control, activity tracking, cost recovery, storage management, security features, and search and retrieval capabilities that were unavailable with the organization's previous system.

countries. A distinctive characteristic of services over products is that a pure service requires simultaneous production and consumption. Instead of competing as domestic industries with business units enjoying high degrees of autonomy, global service industries integrate activities on a worldwide basis to capture linkages between countries. Even today, for most cross-border service transactions to occur, potential buyers in one country must travel to another country. Technology has transformed this requirement by allowing simultaneous production and consumption to occur over telecommunications networks.

There are two trends that are making networking more accessible and, therefore, more important to companies worldwide. First, the worldwide deregulation of telecommunications companies is driving down the cost of bandwidth or capacity. Thus, companies can use wide-area networks in ways they never could before. Whereas sharing information over wide geographic areas was once prohibitively expensive, too slow, or impossible, it needs to now be a part of every company's corporate strategy.

The second trend is the amount of innovation taking place on local area networking technologies. The speeds are increasing dramatically year after year, and the price points for these technologies are decreasing as well. This trend will radically change how people collaborate with services such as desktop video and audio becoming affordable. In addition, architectures for internally developed applications will change, because the need to design around network limitations will be eased.

As these two trends converge, companies can dominate industries by making geography a nonfactor in the effectiveness of the organization. In particular, worldwide economies make most growing business 24-hour operations. Networks allow for people to communicate, data to be passed, product development to be shared, and the latest information to be available when needed.

Stellar Performer:
SABRE

American Airlines successfully maintains a significant competitive advantage in the world market with its Semi-Automated Business Research Environment (SABRE) system. SABRE has been so successful over the years that it has been spun off as a separate entity, now allowed to compete for new IT business. The SABRE network has been a crucial element in the success of American. In fact, American earns a higher ROI by booking tickets than by operating aircraft. The success of SABRE as an entity is that it is built upon a worldwide-connected communications network.

Driven by a need to process large quantities of information during the 1950s and early 1960s, airlines adapted emerging computer technology to develop computerized reservation systems. These systems were dedicated to handling all internal functions of the airline, including booking, ticketing, and scheduling. In the mid-1970s, deregulation was the impetus that pushed the systems to outside users, rather than staying as strictly internal operational tools. Deregulation created a complex environment—fares changed almost hourly, new carriers started service, route structures moved to the hub-and-spoke system (which created scheduling difficulties), and flight schedules were adjusted frequently. Airlines could not keep up with these demands, much less travel intermediaries who operated by calling the airlines directly for information and wrote tickets manually.

To make the concept of customer reservation work at all in this now distributed market, airlines started to use advanced communications technology. Communications technologies allow almost instantaneous transmission of data over cables, lines, and via satellites, to establish automated information networks. Airline computerized reservation systems, like SABRE, are designed to link the producer and user. The SABRE network is vital in providing accurate processing of passenger records. SABRE permits users to access a central database, which contains information on flight availability, schedules, and fares. It features the ability to book flights and prepare tickets, invoices, itineraries, and boarding passes. This unique capability to create a truly global network is highly sought after by airlines and travel intermediaries.

So, how does SABRE take advantage of technology to become a reality? Connected by dedicated data transmission lines, SABRE links its airport operations, headquarters, ticket offices, and travel agency subscribers (who pay a monthly access fee for data and equipment charges for hardware). SABRE is also available directly to consumers

(Continued)

(Continued)

and purchasers of travel via several commercial on-line networks, as it aggressively seeks a position in the home personal computing market. For example, it is relatively easy for a subscriber to America Online to secure access to information, make a reservation, and arrange to have the airline ticket delivered to a home or business address.

SABRE is also an international product that is now relying heavily on the rapidly emerging telecommunications infrastructures of developing nations. Through its global network, American Airlines no longer needs to establish production facilities around the world; it is able to market access to their network anywhere, maintaining production facilities in the United States. As each carrier developed marketing methods to assist market penetration in foreign markets, American primarily exports SABRE directly to users; the user is sold or leased hardware that permits access via telecommunications to the data core in the United States.

The reservation network also ties to the processes of general airline management. It affords the management team the opportunity to lessen the need for face-to-face contact. Monitoring and production levels are done by computers, which transmit data back to headquarters. Decisions can be made more rapidly, using the latest possible data.

Source: Dawne M. Flammger, A Case Study on SABRE (3 May 1995).

Fast Forward to the Real World

Interview with Paul Saffo

Eric Nee

Paul Saffo has the kind of job many people would kill for. He travels around the globe, talking to some of the brightest minds in business and science, in an effort to figure out what the future will bring. Saffo has a solid grounding in history, a deep fascination with new technologies, and a dollop of skepticism that keeps him from flying off into fantasy. He calls himself a forecaster and says his views are agnostic, unlike futurists such as George Gilder. Saffo has been with the Institute for the Future in Menlo Park, California, for 11 of its 28 years. One thing that preoccupies Saffo is, naturally, the future of the Internet, and he spoke at length about it during this interview.

UPSIDE: **Did the rapid acceptance of the Internet over the last year catch you by surprise?** SAFFO: It was just a matter of time before this happened, and it seemed like the Internet would be the most likely thing to trigger it. The Internet, as important as it is, is really just a local phenomenon. The '80s were shaped by the advent of cheap microprocessors, which triggered a decade-long processing revolution. By the end of the decade we'd figured out how to process everything pretty well, and a couple of things happened. Adding more processing power to 1980s processing tasks really amounted to very little except making the computational tasks faster. Now, in the '90s, the thing that is shaping the competitive landscape is the advent of cheap lasers. In each case the initial impact has been on cost. Microprocessors were a big deal because they were so cheap. Lasers were a big deal because they made the cost of storage and communications real cheap. But what happens when you make something really cheap? You use more of it. And that is where the long-term impact will be.

One fundamental difference between the two eras is that the rollout of the microprocessor revolution was unencumbered by governmental intervention. But the communications revolution that could be enabled by optical lasers is

(Continued)

(Continued)

subject to much more government intervention and regulation. To the contrary. It happened, to begin with, because the government did some things right, and it was actually the divestiture of the phone companies, AT&T, that created the communications revolution we have now. We're now in this slushy period where there are a lot of new issues being tossed around. What we really need is a new theory of communications.

What's the next big technology after lasers? Cheap sensors. The first place we're going to see this is with MEMS technology— microelectronic mechanical systems. It basically uses semiconductor fabrication techniques and technologies to create really small devices. Where you're probably going to see it hit our lives first are airbags. Did you know that in some areas, thieves are now targeting airbags in cars as often as stereos? The expensive part of the airbag is the sensor. It's a device the size of a coffee cup. You want to get it right because you don't want it to go off prematurely. It's the best they could do, the best they could miniaturize it, and they cost a lot of money. It will hit Detroit first, but it's going to be in all kinds of places.

Is this the same as nanotechnology? These are micromachines. Nanotech is the next level below. This is down to micron scale. That's still pretty good and it's just an engineering problem. There's no fundamental science involved. It's just a straightforward application resisting engineering design.

Could an office worker use this technology? That's the wrong question. Let's put it this way: How does the advent of cheap and ubiquitous sensors change the environment we're in? Imagine cameras all over the network aimed out at the world, everywhere.

And you just click into them? Or maybe nobody clicks into them at all. The only thing that's watching is a computer. You could throw out a small cluster of sensors that sit out in a terrain. We're starting to see hints of what that future could be like here in the Bay Area, with all the cameras mounted on poles along freeways. At Xerox PARC they played with this years ago, where there was a workstation with a camera and you walked in the room and it said, "Oh, he's in the room." The screen turned itself on and the type on the screen said, "Oh, he's about 15 feet away," so the type on the screen was very large. And as you walked closer, the type got very small until

(Continued)

(Continued)

you were sitting at your desk. It's sort of a researchy thing, but the possibilities are interesting. MEMS is just a footnote. It's just one piece of technology that's going to occur. What we're going to do is figure out how to make really cheap sensory devices replicating ears, eyes, and other senses, and they'll be ubiquitous.

Some people say business on the Internet will result in what is being called friction-free capitalism, because the Internet takes much of the intermediary layer out of the traditional capitalist system. It's a little too pat for my taste. If you look at the larger context, there is no doubt that we are reinventing capitalism. "Friction-free capitalism" makes me uneasy because the way things play out is often counterintuitive. People talk about technology disintermediating, but think about how you might buy a copier. If all this information-technology stuff is true, then Canon would talk to you directly electronically. That doesn't happen. You'd probably buy it from Office Club. You'd buy the copier based on advertisements in XYZ magazine. Then there's the toner, and you would probably buy that from Price Club. If you are a small company, you would probably lease your copier from a reseller. The bottom line here is that it's not a value chain, it's a value web.

The Internet makes it cheap to be an intermediary, so you're going to end up with more intermediaries, not fewer. In fact, that's what knowledge work is. In my more cynical moments, I think that if things keep up and it keeps getting this cheap and effective to become an intermediary, then everybody on the planet is an intermediary and there is one buyer and one seller left.

But if this software allows you to buy directly from United Airlines for a lower price, won't that tend to replace travel agents for many flights? Yes, but would I always do that? Today I buy my business travel tickets from the corporate agent who the Institute for the Future uses. If I'm planning my own vacations, I go a completely different route. Ten years ago I interacted with United two ways, direct or through my travel agent. Now it's myriad ways. That is why the most important metaphors are ecological. In the end, asking the question, "How long is the value chain?" is a little bit like asking the question, "How long is the English coast?" The answer is 1) it depends, and 2) effectively, it's infinite.

If you want to keep measuring it at a more and more micro level. Right. It's one length if you're in a plane flying

(Continued)

(Continued)

around the island of England. It's another one if you're in a boat going in and out of the coves. It's longer yet if you're in a car driving along the bluffs. And it's longest yet if you're an ant climbing up and down over each little rock and pebble. The Internet will allow for a myriad number of ways to intermediate all kinds of interactions. That's been the biggest change between the mass-media age of the '60s and the personal-media age that we're solidly into today. All of our thinking today is infused with theories that there is one way to do things. What is the one optimum way to do things? What is the one outcome?

We seem to be going in two directions at once. On the one hand, some brands, like Disney, are becoming ever more important and dominant on a global scale. But at the same time the number of smaller microbrands is proliferating. There's two aspects to that. One, this notion of brands disappearing is moronic. In an overloaded environment, everybody's going to look for things they can trust, like Disney. At the same time, the brands themselves are becoming more diverse. What Disney stands for today is very different than Disney in 1964. When change clusters at the extreme like that, you have the makings of a real dramatic change ready to happen.

A hundred years from now, are we going to be living in a society that is fundamentally different from capitalism as we know it today, or are the changes going to be less dramatic? First of all, we're not going to have to wait 100 years. I think this is a 50-year phenomenon. One thing that's important to keep in mind about revolutions is that most of the time, it seems quite evolutionary, just getting on with business, except for those moments when some transformative event happens. The Berlin Wall was one of those moments. As the decades accumulate, you discover that all the small, daily changes have had a profound effect.

A number of people have started to talk about the technology haves and have-nots. There was an editorial in the *San Francisco Examiner* recently that criticized Steve Jobs for having made a billion dollars off the Pixar [Animation Studios, Richmond, Calif.] IPO, saying it was time to redistribute that wealth to others. I thought it was a ridiculous editorial, but it reflects a growing feeling among some of

(Continued)

(Continued)

the population that, hey, there are all these people getting rich off this change and they're leaving the rest of us behind. To my mind, what's going to be happening is that there is going to be more equality of opportunity, but the end result is more inequality in results because the Internet will tend to exacerbate any results. It's a really important issue, but they picked the wrong example. Steve Jobs bought what everybody else thought was a bad idea. He spent a lot of money getting into that, and he worked very hard at making it work. And just like everything else, you've got to do it right. He worked very hard, and just because all the money arrived at one point doesn't mean he got rich overnight. He'd been in it for years, and that kind of wealth creation creates other jobs.

Just look at Apple, which Jobs helped create. The Macintosh created tens of thousands of jobs inside and outside of Apple. Yes. But haves and have-nots is a big issue. Mitch Kapor frames it as knows and know-nots. I always wanted a Cray 1 supercomputer for Christmas. The problem is that they take up a lot of space and are kind of expensive, and actually, when it comes down to it, unless you're a meteorologist there's not a lot you can do with it. But this Christmas I will get my wish, because the current crop of video game machines are as powerful as a Cray 1. Yeah, video games are not an ennobling technology, but they do expose kids to computer technology and help them learn to control their environment. So the way through here is to keep making the technology cheaper. How do you fairly and equitably distribute knowledge and access to knowledge and access to the things that you need to be a fully participating and enfranchised member of society? It's everybody's business.

Do you think Silicon Valley pays enough attention to that? Silicon Valley historically has not paid attention to it. Silicon Valley was too immature, too young to realize that it had social obligations. But that's changed. There is a lot of social consciousness coming up and a lot of sense of responsibility spreading out. Now, an exception to this is young Bill Gates, who still, despite all of his wealth, is miserly in terms of the things that he does for charities and social change, and that's a scandal. If his mother were alive, she would paddle him for it, because his parents did better than Bill does. It's inexcusable that he doesn't.

(Continued)

(Continued)

In some ways it's really in their self-interest to do it because there is a risk of a backlash during a period such as this, when people resent the change. That's absolutely true. Self-interest is a funny thing. The first thing that you learn in forecasting is the longer the view you take, the more is in your self-interest. Seemingly altruistic acts are not altruistic if you take a long enough view. In the end, being good and doing the right thing and being socially aware is an act of self-interest. That's why the most important thing that we have to do is to teach people to think about the long-term consequences of their actions. I love that vision of Bill Gates getting paddled by his late mother, and she would have done it too.

The place where the terms "haves" and "have-nots" really does crop up is at an international level. An engineer in Silicon Valley doing software would discover that his competition is not another engineer from Stanford with a house in Cupertino and a mortgage like his. Chances are, it's an engineer in Bombay, or China or the former Soviet Republics, who is a full Ph.D. working for $300 a month. Imagine life in Bombay—that engineer is drawing down a salary that is small by Silicon Valley standards, but very large by the standards of his neighbors. And it's a culture where the infrastructure to pour that money back into the community may not be there yet. Suddenly you have this comparatively wealthy engineer involved in the developed world living cheek by jowl with people who are still stuck in a developing world, and there's no way to jump through into it. That's social dynamite.

In Bombay. Yeah, but it's also social dynamite in the United States. As people using technology start moving out into the countryside, further and further from the big city, without sacrificing city salary—stockbrokers, stock traders who move out to Montana—suddenly you've got someone who gave up their fancy apartment in New York, moves to Montana, drops a couple hundred thousand on a nice piece of land and a house that by neighborhood standards is elaborate, living cheek by jowl with someone who is living in an old double-wide trailer trying to scrape together jobs as best as they can. That is social dynamite.

That's occurring in Rocky Mountain areas like Jackson Hole. And you're seeing it everywhere. Nye County, Nevada, is ground zero for this stuff, where the wise users are fighting the government. It's not safe to be a Forest Service official out there. My

(Continued)

(Continued)

strong suspicion is that it is not really a battle between liberal and conservative, and it's not environmental vs development, though it has those dimensions. This is a battle between rural and urban. And Nye County is basically saying, "We don't want yuppies. You yuppies and your yuppie values just stay in the city and leave this area to us. This is not your land." We're going to see more of that, and information technology is what's triggering it. Wealthy people come in. First they have a computer, then they demand latte and espresso shops, and then they want schools and curbs and all these things.

So how will that play out? In a very ugly, unpredictable way. I think you're going to see some symbolic acts. Just like people fought freeways in the 1960s, you're going to start seeing some communities start saying, AT&T, you are not putting a T1 link into our town. We don't want bandwidth, because we know that if you put bandwidth in our town, the next thing that we're going to get is a bunch of spoiled yuppies from Silicon Valley here crapping up our neighborhood.

You wouldn't anticipate that by reading most of the accounts of this current back-to-the-land movement. It won't be uniform. Telluride, Colorado, has made the decision that it wants to be a high-tech enclave. Then there are other places like Aspen that have become landlocked Monte Carlos. You've got the Bill Joys of this world building mountaintop Shangri-las.

At the same time, this is going to be good for towns that are otherwise unremarkable but in perfectly nice places, like Iowa. Towns that have been shrinking ever since they got passed by the freeway. A lot of people are going to say, "I don't want to live in Bozeman [Montana]. I don't care about fly fishing. I just want to be in a nice rural town with a real community." They will welcome them. But that's also consistent. Again, it's not a mass-media world. It's a personal-media world, where you're going to see good benefits and bad benefits, people opposing and people endorsing all of this. But we will look back at 1995 and laugh at how naive we were when we believed that everybody in small communities thought the communications phenomenon was a good thing.

One of the articles you have written talks about the interplay between culture and technology and how culture helps shape technology. It seems to me that the PC as we know it, and the Internet as we know it, are largely U.S. cultur-

(Continued)

(Continued)

ally defined products. Is the present form that we see it in going to be it? What impact might China or the rest of Asia have on the PC and its evolution, or the Internet and its evolution? Well, we're already seeing it with the Internet. We're really close to breaking out of the ASCII jail. When you break out of that you can have true multimedia requirements. It will be especially interesting in Japan and China, where until now the ideographic writing systems of those countries have been so hard to replicate in electronic environments that they've had to fall back on Roman characters. But now we're able to use Kanji and Kana on electronic devices, and very shortly on the Internet. That localizes with a vengeance. The one constant is the nature of human physiology. You know that on our desktops is going to be something that is screen-like and about 3 feet away from us with a keyboard. After that, inside that universe in a box, it will change. The software is where you are going to become increasingly localized. It's just barely beginning to happen.

Will other cultures find this technology as interesting and compelling as we do? Yes, but they're going to reinvent it for their own ends. Several decades ago Marshall McLuhan observed that the whole world was becoming a global village because of the impact of mass media. Well, McLuhan hit a large nail not quite on the head, as was his wont. In fact, the world is not becoming a single global village. It is becoming multiple, interlinked global villages. That is the difference between mass media and personal media.

Let's talk a little about the $500 Internet terminal that has gotten so many people excited. That one is pretty straightforward. There is still substantial uncertainty around whether or not the $500 box will come to pass. Let me paint a scenario that I think is more than 50 percent probable. Five hundred-dollar terminals will not arrive in 12 months. If they do arrive, they will probably arrive in 18 to 24 months. We'll see some things sooner, but to get into the consumer consciousness [will take longer]. If all goes well, the $500 terminal may be the big Christmas present of 1997. Now, it won't actually cost $500 to make. It will probably cost closer to $1,000 to make because the one limiting factor is the cost of the monitor. But we will buy it for $500 because it will probably be sold to us much in the same way that cell phones are sold today, by companies happily subsidizing the hardware knowing they will sell services.

(Continued)

(Continued)

That would be companies like TCI and AT&T? Those kinds of folks. We pay $500, even though it costs $1,000. We will describe it as a lightweight PC, but in fact it won't be a dumb terminal. When all is said and done, the device two years from now will have all the processing power of at least a high-end PC of today. A couple of things have happened to the World Wide Web in the meantime. The Web as we know it today is dead. It's dead in two ways: because it's going to mutate into something else very quickly and be unrecognizable within 12 months, and secondly, it's dead because all it's got on it is dead information.

So the Web page that *Upside* just spent all this time developing is going to have to be redone in 12 months? Sooner. One reason why publishers love the Web is that it's a perfect simulation of a magazine page. It's two dimensional and it's just dead information lying there on the screen. Sure, there are links, but the links just lead to more dead information. It's a big information mausoleum. But with things like Java, you get animation. The information is alive. You can have applets downloading custom stuff. Second thing is, the Web goes from 2D to 3D with technologies like VRML and QuickTime VR, so that shifts it from being a two-dimensional page to being a three-dimensional space, limited only by issues of how fast you can move data in and out. The third change is the whole community side. Today, if you think about it, it's really quite bizarre. You dial into a Web page. There may be a thousand other people at that page. But the only way that you even know anyone else is there is that the server is slow. The next big change is going to be finding ways to put qualities that we associate with MUDs today into Web pages so that you can interact with people. The one thing that we know is that just making the Internet easy to use is not going to motivate people to pay $500 for this terminal.

Maybe it happens first in Japan for the following reasons: Everybody in Japan is intensely interested in network society issues and the Internet. The installed base of PCs in Japan, however, is very low in consumer households. The Japanese government says it is a national priority to become a networked society. Nippon Telegraph and Telephone says great, we'll lower the rate of ISDN to $40 a month or less. And the cable companies in Japan, who are rapidly building up—Japan has been behind us in terms of cable—say they'll work on cable modems as well. And then the consumer electronics companies, Toshiba looks likely to be the first, already are

(Continued)

(Continued)

licensing Java technology. They come out with the terminals. They sell them like crazy in Japan. And it goes back to the localization issue you mentioned. They're tweaked so that they handle multilingual script, and they do Kanji and other languages. Well, then what's a killer app?

Gaming? Maybe.

They're gaming freaks. Well, you'll see it's a license for obsession. But the real surprise is going to be [that] there is this large population of single women in Japan who have great-paying jobs, but because they're single they are still living at home with their parents, and thus have enormous amounts of [discretionary] income. They're very enthusiastic purchasers of items from American mail-order catalogs. So this becomes the "cybershop until you drop"—a vehicle for Land's End and L.L. Bean to sell stuff to Japan, delivered by some specialized Federal Express prepositioned system.

Then [the Internet terminal] comes back to the United States, after they hit volumes in media in Japan. What's amusing about it, though, if that should come to pass, [is that] it's a return to the 1970s notion of the Japanese taking our great ideas and turning them into profitable products. In the U.S., I really am worried that it's going to get screwed up. There are a couple of things that get in the way of the $500 Internet terminal being exciting. Bandwidth is an issue. ISDN is just too darn slow. It's a scandal.

Meanwhile, the cable companies look like they can give us up to 30-megabit-per-second cable access. The problem is that heaven is where you have cable-style bandwidth with phone company-style discipline. Hell is where you have the bandwidth delivered by the cable companies. We'll get lots of bandwidth, but it probably is bandwidth that will lead only to the annoying banality that characterizes the cable companies.

What about your neighbor here, @Home [a cable-based Internet access company started by Kleiner Perkins Caufield & Byers, the venture capital firm located next to the Institute in Menlo Park, Calif.]? @Home is a key player to watch. But I shudder at the prospect of having [TCI, Inc. CEO John] Malone shape the kind of destinations I can go to on the Internet. TCI is a company that should be ashamed of itself. They go for the least common denominator. Brendan Gill, of *The New Yorker,* made the

(Continued)

(Continued)

observation that what's really wrong with our culture today is that we have become like Rome. We are busily converting everything into entertainment and superstition. The O.J. Simpson trial, thanks to digital technology and the incentives there are in the TV business, was reduced to a circus, utterly drained of any social value. And our sports, thanks to television and the money flowing through it, are no longer sports. They are mere entertainment. They are gladiatorial escapades. And now to allow known offenders, like cable companies and the entertainment industry, to jump in and grab what would be the fastest conduit to this new personal medium, the Internet, is a terrifying social prospect.

But they are the ones with the cable connections running into our homes. In the long run, the phone companies are going to push the same thing through.

But that rollout is going to take a long time. That may be what holds up this $500 Internet terminal thing too, is that the actual rollout of cable modems may be slow. We have yet to see the first cable modem appear in the store available for purchase. It made sense and everybody's building them.

Will that $500 terminal be capable, a year from now or a year and a half from now, of doing the kind of things that one will be able to do on the PC over the Internet? No, because it's going to be doing different things. You'll discover that those $500 Internet terminals actually do some things better than a PC and other things worse. In the long run, the real application is connecting people. It's what's so profoundly wrong with the name "information revolution." There are a lot of things wrong with the phrase, but one of them is that this is not about information. It's about people connected to people. The Web will evolve to a place where, instead of connecting people to information, it connects people to people in information-rich environments. The people who construct those information-rich environments are going to be the ones who get rich three, four or five years from now.

You wrote an article about the hierarchy of consumer desires, which ranked entertainment at the top, ahead of communication. Is what you are saying simply wishful thinking? It's true, the entertainment industry is merely pandering

(Continued)

(Continued)

to human tastes. I'm not suggesting that Hollywood drags us kicking and screaming to tacky, violent films. There's a part of this population that is eager for it and wants more. Entertainment really is the top thing in this.

So is it wishful thinking that the Internet is going to evolve to a way to "communicate in an information-rich environment?" No, people interacting with other people is a form of entertainment. And again, I'm a pure agnostic about how this turns out. I am neither an optimist nor pessimist. The most likely outcome is that we will muddle through and there will be some short-term distortions and things out of control that will sort [themselves] out. That even includes things like pornography. It turns out that every new medium in history that has gone on to be a success has passed through pornography, including books. Pornography is to media what acne is to being a teenager. It's just a part of the growing-up process, and mercifully, as a society, we grow out of it pretty fast.

The Internet is not the end of Western civilization as we know it. It is also not going to deliver us to some sort of new techno-nirvana. Each generation tends to invest its deepest fears and its fondest hopes in the nearest new technology coming on. People are viewing it as the wings of salvation, and also the ultimate destruction of mankind. We will have more and more of that angst, particularly since the year 2000 is approaching rapidly. The closer it gets, the more people are going to go to one extreme or the other.

The millennium phenomenon. The fact is that we all get nervous around New Year's [Eve]. Humans are fascinated with boundaries and will find boundaries even when there aren't any. But the greater the number of zeros there are in the year that's rolling away, the sooner you get nervous, the more nervous you get, and the longer it lasts. Decade endings are the ones that get names. They usually last about six to nine months. At the end of the '60s we called it the Age of Aquarius and at the end of the '80s it was the Harmonic Convergence. Look at the end of the last century. The notion of world-weary sophistication and despair and hope that happened in France and the United States is classic century ending. We haven't been through three zeros lately. In fact, we've never really been through three zeros before, because the last time we were, most people were still using Roman numerals, so it was the dreaded letter M. But it disrupted a century of social history.

(Continued)

(Continued)

When you combine that with the changes that the digital age is bringing on, you're probably compounding the effect. I see a very unharmonic convergence here of digital technologies and the millennium and the ever more entertainment society that we've become. We've also become steadily more superstitious. We're becoming touchingly superstitious. All we need is for some event out of the skies, some meteoroid or some dramatic thing. We are already well into a 10-year silly season leading up to the millennium.

Should we all move to Alaska? No. A fundamentalist friend of mine said to me, with a completely straight face, "There is no point in moving anywhere because it's going to affect us all."

I meant to escape the chaos. The wackos. Well, we're all going to go just a little bit crazy.

And with the Internet, any crazy notion is going to be widely disseminated quickly. The Internet is a fabulously rich environment for spreading our fears.

One thing that we haven't touched on is intellectual property and copyrights, and the value of ideas and information. Some people think digital technology is going to make copyrights unenforceable. Other people are saying quite the contrary, that this is going to be an information-based society and the only way it is going to be able to function is if we can enforce copyrights and realize value out of it. People lament the fact that the law is lagging behind the technology. We should all get over that. The only time the law does a worse job than [lagging] behind the technology is when the laws are created in advance of the technology. There is still a constant to intellectual property, and that is that copyright laws have always been the icing on top of a technological fact. And the technological fact was that the best way to protect something is to make it hard to duplicate. The real copyright protection of books was that it was cheaper to buy the book than to replicate it. Digital technologies at the moment are easy to replicate, and we all know that. But as we elaborate these technologies, it's going to get harder to replicate them. We will work it out in the business environment first, in real time, and it will be a messy process. People will get sued. Other people will lose money, other peo-

(Continued)

(Continued)

ple will make money as we work out a collective consensus about what's the appropriate model for balancing the need to make information available and also balancing the need to keep information owned, so that you continue to have an incentive to create more stuff.

So you do think that there will still be something like copyright that allows me to own the stuff that I created, put it out there, and go after somebody if they take it when I don't want them to? I think there will be. The whole modern notion goes back several centuries. This elaborate and delicate structure is held together by legal spit and chickenwire. You will see a fundamental overturn. The thing that's missing is that we need people to provide new theoretical frameworks that really fit the environment. Wired lists Marshall McLuhan as a patron saint. That is a testament to the intellectual impoverishment of life in the digital age, that we have to look to dead, white-boy visionaries from the 1960s for our inspiration. We desperately need thinkers to set new intellectual structures, not just in copyrights and intellectual property, but in thinking about what the effect of this is on society.

I'm amazed that the people who are thinking about the digital phenomenon are still people who largely grew up in it. There is still a real schism between the digital community and the rest of the world. This is the normal state of affairs.

It is. I shouldn't get frustrated. You should, because that's also a part of the process. Change is extraordinarily slow, even today in this digital world, because in fact change occurs at the speed of thought, not at the speed of electronics. Technology enables, it creates options and opportunities, but change is actually effected by the actions of individuals, acting alone, in communities and ultimately as entire cultures. And the lesson, even from the other media of this century, is that it takes about a decade for the innovation to begin in earnest. So all this excitement that we're seeing on the Internet today, while it's all wonderful, the main event is yet to come. E-mail is quaint, horseless-carriage technology, and the World Wide Web is in its own way quaint horseless-carriage technology, imitating what we've got in magazine pages. This is the Bakelite phase of the medium. Bakelite was the first plastic. Everybody spent their time trying to make it look like wood and tortoise shell because they

(Continued)

(Continued)

weren't comfortable with it looking like plastic. But after about a decade, people realized that it made crummy phony wood and tortoise shell. It was really much more sensible to just allow it to be plastic as a medium in its own right, and then plastics got interesting. Well, the Web simulating magazine pages is the Bakelite phase of the Internet.

Why is it that the terms that are used to describe people who are into digital technology, like nerds and cyberpunks, are all sort of derogatory? The kids who were raised on Nintendo machines are barely out of law school at this point. They need two or three more years before they have influence. The simple fact is that in a world of stubborn people, people just don't change. They just grow old.

So it's going to take a new generation to come up? Yeah. It takes about 30 years for any really new idea to be fully embedded in our culture as an unremarkable fact of life. I don't mean that nothing happens for 30 years, it's just that there are 10 years of, in effect, paving the cowpaths—using the technology to do some old thing in a slightly different way. E-mail is a cowpath-paving application. The second decade is the decade of the entrepreneurs—the people with the shoestring budgets, crazy ideas and not a lot of adult supervision. The third decade is when we really integrate it into society. As far as the Internet is concerned, we're still in that first 10-year period.

But the digital phenomenon in general is in the second, if not third decade. Oh yeah, that's true. Treat that 30-year pattern as a heuristic, not a hard-and-fast rule, and then the issue is, which technology do you look at? The closer you get to something that's an actual product for consumers, the more useful it is. But we are going to be more surprised by the Internet in the next five years than in the last five years, and the surprises will not all be pleasant. Internet mavens will be shocked and disappointed by what the cable companies do to it as a price of getting a big hunk of access over cable. Other people, Internet skeptics, will be amazed at how quickly this thing diffuses out into the culture. The essence of the Internet is that it represents a profound shift in the nature of communications. It's a shift from doing communications as a conduit, a pipe between physical locations on the planet, to viewing communications as a destination in its own right.

(Continued)

(Continued)

So you're more skeptical about the transformative powers of the Internet. People like John Perry Barlow talk about the Web taking us closer to God. Barlow is a visionary, not a forecaster, and this is an ecology where we need all kinds of folks. I love many of Barlow's visions. Other of Barlow's visions horrify me. But he's a visionary. George Gilder's a visionary. These are people who are out there on the edge, trying to live it and point us to the options. They are the pathfinders.

While there will be profound transformations, it will also be a lot more like today than it is different. For example, if you wander into someone's house 10, 15 years from now, at first it will look no different than it does now. Where you will get staggered and surprised by the scale of differences is in the details. How devices are used, what's actually in those devices will have changed. It's important to remember that people are extraordinarily conservative, and anyone who doubts that should just drive around Orange County and look at all the pseudo-Tudor English houses or French Provincial houses.

As the editor of this magazine who's also responsible for our on-line presence, I would in some ways prefer that the Web had not happened. I like magazines, and I'd just as soon keep publishing the magazine and not have to worry about an on-line presence and what that's going to do to the magazine. I'm at a bit of a disadvantage compared to an 18-year-old who's all gung-ho about the Web. You can take comfort from the fact that we all feel the same way. And guess what? That 18-year-old will feel the same way after he's all invested in his thing. Mark Twain put it very nicely when he said, "You know, I'm all for progress, but it's change that I don't like." Most people have this idea of change that really comes down to changing everything except the space that they stand on. They want the whole world transformed to preserve their old habit. That's in human nature. That is why, in fact, change is occurring so slowly. But a lot of people are saying, wait a minute, life is changing more quickly and is more unpredictable than it was in the past. There is this funny acceleration effect that comes from the fact that even though the individual components are all changing as slowly as ever, more things are changing at once. It's the intersection of two-decades-old trends that led to the explosion of the Internet. One was the increase in bandwidth over telecommunications lines, and the other one was the evolution of the Internet itself.

(Continued)

(Continued)

How will this play out in the next couple years? What will happen is the $500 terminal will take a little longer to arrive. We've already seen people knocking the Internet, pointing out that there is no value to it and all that. In 12 months people will be off of it completely. It's not going to disappear because there is too much value in it and companies really are providing real productivity benefits. But it's going to be a little tiresome. And it will be safe within 12 months to admit that you don't have a personal home page, or can't use a PC.

Source: Eric Nee, "Interview with Paul Saffo," Upside magazine (February 1996).

Editor's Note: Eric Nee, formerly editor of Upside magazine, is now Silicon Valley bureau chief for Forbes magazine. Paul Saffo continues as a director of the Institute for the Future and is one of the most respected pundits in the technology world.

Measuring Workplace Performance with IT

Craig Kaplan, IQ Company

Chief executive officers invest in total quality management (TQM) programs, because they want to improve the bottom line. They are betting that TQM will lead to higher profits, either by reducing costs or increasing revenue from more satisfied customers. For example, TQM efforts at IBM's largest software development site began in earnest when a new general manager discovered that 60 to 80 cents of every development dollar was being spent on software maintenance and rework. Total quality management represented an opportunity to reduce these costs.

In IBM's case, the TQM investment paid off. Figure A.1 summarizes the results achieved between 1989 and 1993. The primary goal of cost savings was realized with service costs decreasing by 20 percent. At the same time, revenues grew as customer satisfaction with key products increased 14 percent relative to competitors. Underlying these financial results were more than 40 leadership, process, and technology improvement techniques that enabled IBM to reduce its software defect levels by 46 percent and increase revenue per employee by 56 percent. Together, these factors helped IBM's largest software site remain profitable at a time when much of the rest of the company was experiencing financial distress. Team-based quality assess-

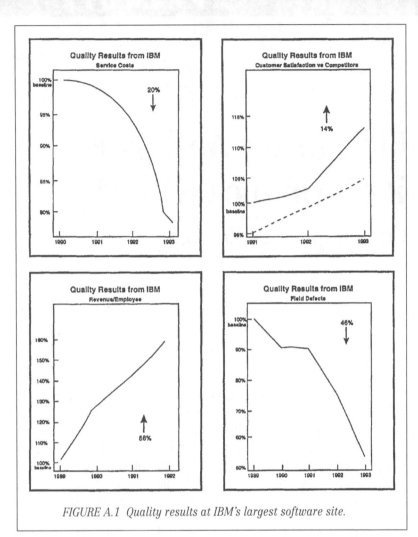

FIGURE A.1 Quality results at IBM's largest software site.

ments were probably the most important element of IBM's successful TQM effort.

WHY YOU NEED COMPUTERIZED, TEAM-BASED ASSESSMENTS

Quality assessments help organizations form a clear idea of where they are and of what they need to improve. Team-based assessments provide a more accurate view than a single assessor can; foster buy-in, because they involve more people; and help organizations track progress over time and maintain focus. Compared with low-tech assessment methods, computerized assessments take less time and fewer resources and are more effective.

Which quality assessment criteria an organization chooses is less important than its commitment to involve the entire organization in the assessment, and to follow up each assessment with concrete quality improvement actions. It should, however, choose an assessment that matches its goals. If the goal is quality improvement on a broad scale, an organization might consider the Malcolm Baldrige National Quality Award criteria or other state quality award criteria that are based on Baldrige. If the focus is primarily on process, or if the organization needs quality certification, the ISO 9000 series might be a logical choice. Finally, there are quality assessments and models for specific industries, such as the Software Engineering Institute's CMM model for the software industry.

IBM chose the Malcolm Baldrige National Quality Award criteria as its primary quality assessment tool, because the Baldrige criteria are so comprehensive. The seven Baldrige categories cover all aspects of a business, from leadership to process improvement and from business results to customer satisfaction. Although IBM's largest software site also sought (and obtained) ISO 9001 registration, ISO is much narrower in scope than Baldrige. In fact, at the time of the IBM site's ISO registration, most of the scope of ISO 9001 could fit within the scope of a few of the 1994 Baldrige categories (Figure A.2).

Once an organization chooses an assessment, the real work begins. Sound management practice combined with appropriate use of technology can help it overcome obstacles and sustain a successful quality improvement effort.

TECHNOLOGY AND THE SEVEN CHALLENGES TO QUALITY ASSESSMENT

Most large organizations will face assessment challenges in the following seven areas. Combined with strong leadership, IT—specifically team-based assessment software—can help an organization successfully meet these challenges.

Challenge 1: Gaining Commitment

Leadership plays the central role in gaining buy-in, whereas technology plays a supporting part.

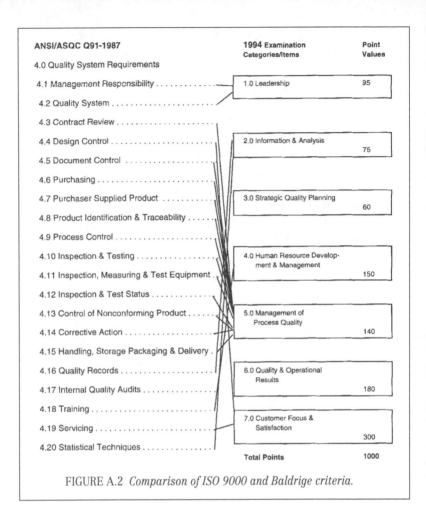

FIGURE A.2 *Comparison of ISO 9000 and Baldrige criteria.*

For a large-scale quality improvement effort to have a reasonable chance of success, senior management must be committed. Typically, commitment at the senior level comes because these executives realize that cost savings and other competitive advantages will accrue from sustained quality improvement efforts. But even once benefits are understood intellectually, true buy-in does not occur until everyone begins implementing and taking personal responsibility for quality improvement. Commitment follows involvement. Technology simply makes involvement easier in the same way that it's easier to convince people to help you build a house if you allow them the option of using power tools instead of insisting that everything be done by hand.

Periodic assessments are a tried-and-true method of getting everyone involved. At IBM, one site general manager insisted on quarterly management reviews of quality improvement activities. Similarly, the U.S. Air Force conducts periodic quality self-assessments of Air Force units worldwide. Other organizations—ranging from the city of Austin, Texas, to AT&T—use periodic quality assessments not only to gain information, but also to raise awareness and gain buy-in to improvement efforts.

The most specialized power tools in the assessment world are computerized team assessment products. Most assessment software supports automatic scoring and graphing of results and enables the user to easily enter comments and other information that support the scores (Figure A.3). These standard features reflect an emphasis on increasing efficiency by eliminating the drudgery involved in calculating scores or creating reports with comments and graphs. However, new assessment software programs are also beginning to address issues that affect effectiveness, such as relevance and team participation.

Unfortunately, there is a relevance gap between the generic wording of most popular assessment criteria (for example, Baldrige or ISO 9000 series) and the specific day-to-day activities of an organization. Unless managers bridge this relevance gap in a meaningful way, they will get resistance instead of buy-in.

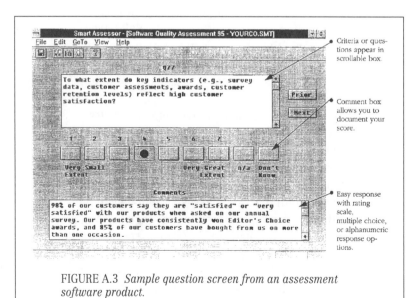

FIGURE A.3 *Sample question screen from an assessment software product.*

Training is an effective but expensive way of bridging the gap. However, in addition to teaching the organization the language of the criteria, many government and private organizations are beginning to adapt the criteria's language *to the organization.* The trend can be seen in the proliferation of state quality awards, almost all of which are modeled on the Baldrige award, but many of which have been adapted to fit the specific needs of a state's applicants. Companies do the same thing. For example, at IBM the sometimes obtuse language of the Baldrige criteria was routinely translated into terms that software developers could understand. Even federal organizations, which are committed to the Baldrige Award, often modify the wording to better fit their constituencies. For example, the U.S. Air Force uses Baldrige as the basis for its "Unit Self-Assessments." However, the wording is often customized to reflect the military character of the Air Force (for example, substituting "base commander" for "senior executive").

New assessment software can help bridge the relevance gap in two ways. First, some assessment software includes on-line notes and advice that help interpret the criteria. This trend parallels the proliferation of books by consultants aimed at helping organizations make sense out of the different assessment criteria. Second, some assessment software packages can be rapidly customized to include notes, changes to question wording, or even new questions and point values in accordance with an organization's needs. Software assessments that include extensive on-line help and that allow customization help increase buy-in to the overall assessment process by bridging the relevancy gap.

Because buy-in follows involvement, assessment software that supports participation by teams also helps deepen commitment within the organization. One of the difficulties with many assessment software packages is that they implicitly assume that a single assessor will be completing the assessment. But, even if a single assessor were able to complete an accurate assessment, the single-assessor approach implies that quality is the responsibility of a single individual, for example, the quality assurance manager. In reality, quality improvement efforts are much more successful if they are approached as team-based efforts requiring everyone's involvement.

Team-based assessment software allows organizations to merge the scores and comments from many assessors, and even from many teams of assessors, into a combined assessment. Team-based software also allows managers to read comments from different assessors, view average scores from all the assessors, and export the comments and scores in a form suitable for editing into a final report. Whereas organizations previously used a combination of spreadsheets, databases, and word processors to conduct team assessments, many groups from the U.S. Air Force, Siemens, and AT&T are now using team-based assessment software to achieve the same effect more easily.

Challenge 2: Communication Technology

The good news is that many of the communications technologies that facilitate quality assessments are already being used by most organizations. For example, E-mail is a natural way to share information among team members conducting assessments, especially if the people involved are in different physical locations.

Many organizations approach the task of a Baldrige assessment by dividing the seven categories among seven team leaders. Each team leader works with several people, and information is shuttled back and forth using E-mail and electronic transfer of word-processing documents and spreadsheets. Within this general team-based approach, variations are possible. For example, IBM used many cross-functional teams, each responsible for conducting a complete Baldrige assessment in a particular product or process area. Then all of the assessments were rolled into one overall assessment for the entire site.

As the scope of the assessment effort increases, communication technology becomes increasingly important, because it becomes increasingly difficult to communicate directly, face-to-face. Thus, in addition to E-mail, IBM set up electronic bulletin boards to allow anyone at the site to comment on quality improvement issues. The site general manager often personally responds to posts on the bulletin boards.

Everyday communication technologies, such as teleconferencing, videotaping, and photocopying, can also play an important role in improving communication in large-scale assessment efforts. AT&T used teleconferences to gather input from team members in different locations. One IBM site used to videotape its quarterly Baldrige assessment presentations and went so far as to broadcast several of them live, throughout the site. Surprisingly, one of the most effective vehicles for raising awareness about specific quality innovations at IBM was a humble newsletter produced by one person who knew lots of programmers with good ideas. He got the programmers to write up what they were doing. Then he edited the articles, photocopied them, and distributed them throughout the site. The articles proved to be a valuable source of information that helped assessment teams understand what activities were going on in parts of the site outside their normal experience.

Beyond the general communication technologies just mentioned, organizations may want to consider two less common approaches that can greatly enhance and focus communication among assessment team members. The first approach, computer-supported team workspaces, was originally developed by IBM to help teams of programmers accomplish their work more effectively. The concept worked so well that it was borrowed by teams of all sorts, including IBM's assessment team members, who used it to help write the site's 70-page Baldrige report.

IBM's approach was to enhance a meeting room by adding a computer with the capability to project the computer screen on the wall. Assessment teams gathered in the room to review drafts of the assessment document, which were projected directly from the computer to a large wall screen. People's comments, suggestions, and notes were added directly to the document during the meeting. Consensus was achieved on phrasing, and, in some cases, missing data or information could be directly brought up on the computer from other sources that were electronically linked to it.

An internal IBM study estimated that the site could save up to 15 percent of its direct labor costs by conducting design sessions, code reviews, document reviews, and other team-oriented meetings in the computer-supported team workspaces.

Much of the savings resulted from the fact that changes could be made and consensus reached during the meeting, instead of requiring additional meetings to review changes later. Subjectively, there is something powerful about seeing ideas immediately captured and documented on a big screen. Some of the brainstorming sessions went on so long that the joke was that the participants ran out of air (because the computer generated heat in the enclosed room) long before they ran out of ideas.

Although IBM eventually built special ergonomic rooms for its computer-supported team workspaces, you don't need a fancy room to try out the idea. At your next meeting, just hook up a computer to an LCD projection panel on top of an overhead projector. Open the assessment document on your computer, and ask a member of the group to make changes to the document and type comments from the group as they arise in discussion. The fact that the group can see the changes immediately on the projected screen creates an effective feedback loop. The miscommunication and misunderstandings that inevitably develop when each person takes his or her own notes disappear as group members debate over what is on the projected screen, clarifying points and ideally reaching consensus. Perhaps the most satisfying aspect of this approach is that the team can leave the meeting having made actual changes in the work product—a rarity in many corporate circles.

A second approach that can be used to improve communication among team members is to cross-reference assessment items. For example, one of the communication problems that almost all Baldrige teams encounter is the issue of determining links between different items of the Baldrige criteria. One team member might be the leader for Category 5, which includes the item "management of supplier performance," while another team member might be focusing on Category 6, which includes the item "supplier performance results." These two team members need to talk so they can avoid duplication of effort and share information.

The U.S. Air Force solved the linkage problem by creating a series of tables that cross-referenced related Baldrige items. The same approach has been incorporated into team-based assessment software used by the Air Force. Nicknamed

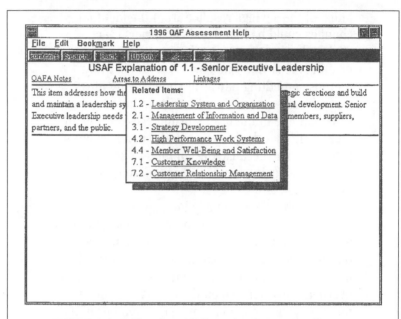

FIGURE A.4 *Golden thread links in the Air Force quality assessment software.*

"golden threads," hypertext links allow assessors to instantly jump to descriptions of all the items related to the one they are currently working on (Figure A.4). In a merged assessment containing the scores and comments of an entire team, the golden threads allow team members to quickly compare everyone's scores and comments for all related assessment items.

Challenge 3: Skills and Training

Even if organizations customize their assessment criteria to make it maximally relevant to them, they are going to have to provide some level of assessment training. Although it is hard to beat a good human instructor for effectiveness, good instructors also tend to be costly. For example, a two-day class with a Baldrige examiner can easily run $10,000 plus expenses.

Less costly alternatives include joining non-profit associations that make training available to their members (for example, the Council for Continuous Improvement), purchasing videotaped training, or relying on a variety of computerized options, ranging from computer-based training programs to on-line tutorials and the on-line help built into assessment software programs.

Internet surfers might want to peruse Baldrige information that is available free of charge from the National Institute of Standards and Technology (http://www.nist.gov). Other useful sites are the American Society for Quality Control (http://www.asqc.org), which points to a variety of other quality improvement sources, and I.Q. Company's site (http://www.iqco.com), which features a free, searchable database of quality-related resources and referral information.

A common training strategy is to provide team leaders with intensive formal assessment training and then have these leaders informally train the other team members. Because the quality and quantity of training varies with this approach, it is a good idea to ensure that the assessment software includes adequate scoring guidelines and assessment help. Otherwise, the scores and comments provided by the team members will vary so widely that consensus will be difficult to achieve. In short, the objective is to ensure that enough training is provided (electronically or otherwise) so that there is consistency in the way teams are interpreting the criteria and scoring the organization.

Challenge 4: Validity

Related to the issue of scoring consistency is the concept of validity. For a self-assessment to be valid, it must capture the views of a representative sample of the organization's population. It should also be based on objective data rather than on subjective opinion or "gut feel." Usually anchoring scores in objective data—that is, increasing the validity of the score—also leads to more consistent scoring. For this reason, an improvement in scoring consistency, when accompanied by data supporting the scores, can indicate an improvement in validity as well.

Senior managers are especially notorious for scoring organizations as they think the organization should be, rather than as the organization actually is. Tempering the vision of senior management with concrete data and the views of others in the organization helps provide an accurate assessment of the organization's true quality maturity.

Sometimes it is even helpful to ask assessors outside the organization to participate, because they tend to have a less-biased view. By tracking scores of various groups over several periodic assessments, you can see whether the scores begin to converge. If they do converge, as they did in IBM's case (Figure A.5), it is probably a good indication that the teams conducting the assessment are developing a better understanding of the criteria and are beginning to score more consistently. This is especially true if one of the groups doing the scoring consists of highly trained individuals, for example, Baldrige examiners, whose scores can be assumed to have a relatively high degree of validity.

Technology can help by automating the process of combining many diverse points of view and providing mechanisms for capturing objective data. In years past, spreadsheets and word-processing programs were the primary means of averaging scores, capturing comments, and producing reports and graphs. Today, team-based assessment software performs many of the same functions in one integrated package. For example, team-based software can help focus attention on areas in which assessors disagree by plotting the scores of different assessors (or teams of assessors) on the same graph (Figure A.6). Items with sharply divergent scores probably need more examination. Some assessment software not only averages scores from many assessors, but it also calculates statistics that quantitatively show where assessors agree and disagree. The advantage of

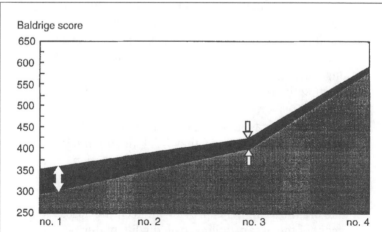

FIGURE A.5 Convergence of scores from two groups of assessors at IBM over four successive Baldrige self-assessments.

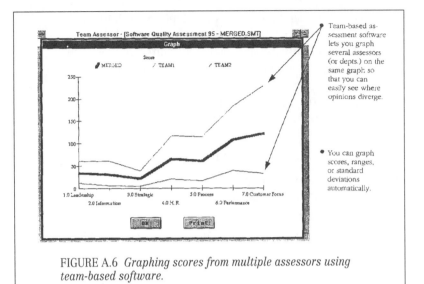

FIGURE A.6 *Graphing scores from multiple assessors using team-based software.*

such statistics is that they, like the graph in Figure A.6, help focus discussion and attention on the areas in which there seems to be the most disagreement.

During the discussion and consensus process, assessors learn from colleagues who scored the organization differently. Ideally, the consensus process improves the validity of the assessment, not simply through compromise, but by bringing to light new facts known previously to only some of the assessors.

The best assessment software goes beyond merely asking for a numerical score. Most criteria require assessors to document and justify scores by providing data and evidence that a particular criterion has been satisfied. The assessment software should provide a means (for example, a large-capacity comment box) for capturing notes and other data that support the score. Ideally, the software should support the capability to incorporate graphics, images, and tables directly into the assessment. In the absence of such features, however, it should be possible at least to export assessment information to other programs that support graphical linking, such as Microsoft Word.

Challenge 5: Cost

The major cost of any large-scale assessment effort is the time of the people involved. The cost of technology that can increase the efficiency of the assessment effort typically pales by comparison. For example, consider the case of IBM's largest software site. Using estimated figures published in the book *Secrets of Software Quality* and the assumption of a burdened labor rate of $100,000 per person-year, we get the following estimated time cost:

Number of person-years expended in four quarterly Baldrige assessments	72
Number of additional person-years expended to secure ISO 9001 registration	50
Total number of person-years	122
Total estimated time cost	122 P.Y.
× $100,000/P.Y.	$12.2 million[1]

Compare this figure of $12.2 million with typical costs for team-based assessment software for Baldrige, plus the incremental cost for adding an ISO 9001 module:

Cost for a single-user, team-based Baldrige assessment software license	$600
Cost for a single-user license for additional ISO 9001 assessment	$200
Total software cost/user	$800
Number of licenses required (10 percent of site population)	180

Total estimated software cost = 180 × $800 = $144 thousand

The cost of team-based assessment software is roughly 1 percent of the cost of the overall time involved in conducting four assessments. Even if the software provided only a 10-percent increase in efficiency, which is low by most estimates, an organization could save ten dollars in personnel costs for every dollar invested in assessment software. More important, the assessment would be easier to conduct and more valid, because it could include more people.

Challenge 6: Improvement

Strictly speaking, assessments are designed to tell organizations where they are, not necessarily what they should do to improve. In fact, Baldrige makes a specific point of emphasizing that the criteria are not prescriptive. And yet, pragmatically, there is not much point in doing an assessment unless managers plan to take the next steps to actually improve. The ISO 9000 series incorporates the notion of corrective action requests, which address this issue. But the organization is left to its own devices when it comes to figuring out which corrective actions to take.

As a response to the need to take steps toward quality improvement, several software companies have developed products that target process improvement. There are flowcharting tools, brainstorming tools, database tools for managing teams, reengineering tools, tools for creating cause-and-effect diagrams, and tools for creating control charts and graphs. Many of these tools have been integrated into quality improvement suites. It is possible to buy quality improvement tool kits separately or bundled with assessment software.

Some assessment software even includes a built-in database of quality improvement resources. Depending on the assessment score, the software automatically retrieves recommended titles of books, articles, software, or other resources from the built-in database. The user clicks on titles of interest to view resource abstracts (Figure A.7). The software even allows the addition of new resources to the database that might be of particular interest to the organization using the assessment. For example, the U.S. Air Force uses assessment software that includes a customized database with

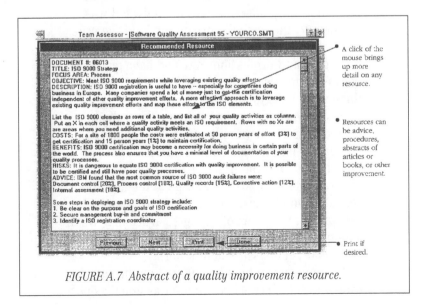

FIGURE A.7 Abstract of a quality improvement resource.

material specific to the Air Force. Other organizations can request inclusion of descriptions of their key quality policies and procedures as related to various categories of an assessment.

It is possible to use both team-based assessment software with built-in improvement resources and specific follow-on tools, such as flowcharting or brainstorming software. The key point is that for an assessment to be most effective, there should be a link between the result of the assessments and the steps that will lead to actual improvement.

Challenge 7: Staff Burnout and Transitions to New Assessments

One of the most serious challenges to IBM's TQM efforts was the burnout of employees who had worked many months on quality improvement without being able to see clear results. Unfortunately, there is a lag between when a process is first improved and when new products created with the improved process finally reach customers. Depending on the length of the product cycle, that time lag can be two years or more—a long time to wait in corporate America.

Periodic assessments help ameliorate this problem, because the assessments typically give credit for changes in processes well before financial results of these changes are apparent. During IBM's four-year quality improvement journey, there was a point—between year 2 and 3—when the main thing that kept the site motivated was the steadily increasing score on the Baldrige criteria. Without that internal gauge of progress, many managers and professionals would have given up, because it took several years (Figure A.1) for financial results to appear.

A related challenge is managing the transition from one assessment to another. Transitions can be minor—for example, shifting from 1994 Baldrige to 1995 Baldrige. Or they can be major—for example, going from Baldrige to the ISO 9000 series. In both cases, there is likely to be some resistance to the idea of change, particularly when a lot of effort and training has gone into learning a particular set of assessment criteria.

Technology can help by automating the switch from one set of criteria to another as much as possible. For example, the U.S. Air Force has developed a formula, which can be implemented on a spreadsheet, for estimating a 1995 Baldrige score based on the 1994 score. Some assessment software programs have gone a step further by incorporating an estimation capability that automatically estimates scores on one assessment based on scores on another related assessment. For example, you might estimate performance on an ISO 9001–based assessment using scores on 1996 Baldrige. The advantage, of course, is that you are able to leverage past work to help you with the new assessment; you need not start completely from scratch. However, there is an important caveat that must be applied to all such estimation approaches: The accuracy of the estimated results depends on the degree of overlap (correlation) between the two assessments in question. Thus, as we saw earlier in Figure A.2, it would be foolish to expect an accurate estimate of performance on Baldrige's business results category based on an ISO 9001 assessment, because ISO 9001 has very little to say about business results.

Provided that assessment software includes estimates only where they are appropriate, the estimation feature can add value and help reduce the feeling of frustration that occurs when an organization switches from one assessment to another. In the case of two assessments that have a high degree of overlap—for example, 1995 Baldrige and 1996 Baldrige, or 1996 Baldrige and a Baldrige-based state or city quality award—estimation capability may be especially useful.

Finally, it is worth emphasizing that much of the data and supporting comments that are gathered for one assessment often apply to other assessments as well. For example, preparing for ISO 9001 registration at IBM was much easier because of all the work that had been done previously for the periodic Baldrige assessments. It is healthy to try a variety of assessments, *provided* that you stick with each long enough to actually get results. The spirit of continuous improvement is to never rest content. No assessment is perfectly complete, so if the organization seems to be doing quite well by one set of criteria, perhaps it is time to try another set.

THE VALUE OF LONG-TERM COMMITMENT

Periodic team-based assessments should be at the heart of any serious quality improvement program. They are an excellent way to gain buy-in across the organization and help the organization focus its improvement efforts. Perhaps most important, they provide the in-process feedback that gives people confidence to stay with the quality improvement journey, even though financial results may be several years away.

Team-based assessment software is a highly cost-effective approach to periodic self-assessment. A typical cost analysis shows that it is reasonable to expect at least ten dollars of cost savings in labor for every dollar invested in team-based software. Team-based software can also improve the effectiveness of the assessment. By averaging scores and merging comments from many assessors, team-based software increases the validity of a self-assessment at the same time that it increases involvement and understanding. Customizable assessment software, particularly if the software has extensive on-line help and assessment advice, can help team members easily see the relevance of the information they are tracking to their day-to-day jobs. The ability to estimate scores on one assessment by using scores on a related assessment can leverage the assessment effort and ease the transition from using one set of assessment criteria to another. Computerized team-based assessments also complement a large number of existing technologies that have greatly helped past assessment efforts. These include E-mail, electronic bulletin boards, the Worldwide Web, spreadsheet/database/word-processing files, teleconferencing, and computer-supported team workspaces.

Although computer-based team assessments can be a tremendous help in carrying out an assessment program, it is important to remember that assessments can be successful only if they are part of a long-term, committed effort to improve quality, as opposed to a "program of the month." The cartoonist Scott Adams captured the distinction very well in a "Dilbert" comic strip that recently appeared in the journal of the American Management Association. In the strip, Dilbert has been asked by his boss to help the company apply for the "Millard Bullrush Quality Award." Under duress, Dilbert pops open his laptop computer, teams up with Dogbert, and says, "I have to submit my project for a 'Quality' award. I'll need your help on the dishonest parts."

Like Dilbert, we can team up and use the latest technology to help with our assessments. However, our toughest challenges may be whether we have the courage to be objective and the commitment to stick with quality improvement long enough to reap the rewards.[2]

Craig Kaplan is CEO of I.Q. Company, a software development and consulting company based in Santa Cruz, California, serving more than 175 client organizations including IBM, AT&T, Siemens, and the U.S. Air Force. Coauthor of *Secrets of Software Quality: 40 Innovations From IBM* (McGraw-Hill, 1995), he is a member of the American Society for Quality Control, Association for Computing Machinery, American Psychological Association, American Management Association, Institute of Electrical and Electronics Engineers, and the Scientific Research Society, Sigma Xi.

INTRODUCTION

1. *Information Week* (June 23, 1997): 10.

CHAPTER 1

1. Paul Strassmann, *The Business Value of Computers* (New Canann, Conn.: Information Executive Press, 1990).

CHAPTER 2

1. *CIO* Magazine (15 April 1997).

CHAPTER 3

1. Daniel P. Petrozzo, *Successful Reengineering.* (Van Nostrand Reinhold, 1994).

2. RHI Consulting, *Information Week* (29 September 1997).

CHAPTER 4

1. This chapter is based on an article that I wrote in 1995 for *National Productivity Review,* published by John Wiley & Sons, Inc. This chapter is adapted entirely from that article. It has been modified to include updates relevant in 1997. Daniel P. Petrozzo, *National Productivity Review,* 1995.

2. Ed Yourdon, *Decline and Fall of the American Programmer.*

3. Peter Drucker, *Post-Capitalist Society.*

CHAPTER 5

1. *Harvard Business Review.*

2. *CIO* magazine (June 1996).

3. *CIO* magazine (15 April 1997).

4. *Information Week* (22 September 1997).

5. *CIO* magazine (June 1996).

6. *Information Week* (29 September 1997).

7. *Information Week* (29 September 1997).

CHAPTER 6

1. Eileen C. Shapiro, *Fad Surfing in the Boardroom: Reclaiming the Courage to Manage in the Age of Instant Answers* (Addison-Wesley Publishing, 1995).

2. *CIO* magazine (June 1996).

3. Theodore Kinni, *America's Best: Industry Week's Guide to World-Class Manufacturing Plants.*

4. Henry Lasker and David Norton, "The New CIO/CEO Partnership."

CHAPTER 7

1. Jack Shaw, www.computerworld.com (posted 14 October 1996).

2. *Information Week* (9 June 1997)

3. *CIO* magazine (October 1996).

4. *CIO* magazine (October 1996).

5. Source: Gartner Group.

6. Source: Stefan Morschheuser and Heinz Raufer, *Proceedings of the 29th Hawaii International Conference on System Sciences* (Los Alamitos, Calif.: IEEE Computer Society Press, 1996), V: 4–13.

APPENDIX

1. *Secrets of Software Quality.*

2. Excerpted from: Craig Kaplan, "Technology to Ease Team-Based Quality Assessments," *National Productivity Review,* 4, No. 3 (Summer 1996): 65–82.